Robert Story

The Lyrical and other minor Poems of Robert Story

With a Sketch of his Life and Writ ngs

Robert Story

The Lyrical and other minor Poems of Robert Story
With a Sketch of his Life and Writings

ISBN/EAN: 9783744776639

Printed in Europe, USA, Canada, Australia, Japan

Cover: Foto ©Thomas Meinert / pixelio.de

More available books at **www.hansebooks.com**

THE LYRICAL

AND OTHER

MINOR POEMS

OF

ROBERT STORY,

WITH A

SKETCH OF HIS LIFE AND WRITINGS.

BY

JOHN JAMES, F.S.A.,

AUTHOR OF THE "HISTORY OF BRADFORD;" "HISTORY OF THE
WORSTED MANUFACTURE IN ENGLAND;" "LIFE OF
NICHOLSON, THE AIREDALE POET," ETC.

LONDON:
LONGMAN, GREEN, LONGMAN, AND ROBERTS;
AND
HENRY GASKARTH, BRADFORD.

1861.

TO THE MOST NOBLE

Algernon,

DUKE OF NORTHUMBERLAND, K.G.

&c. &c. &c.

My Lord Duke,

It is deemed most fitting by the biographer and friends of Robert Story—as it certainly would have been the wish of the Bard himself—that this Volume should be dedicated to your Grace.

Your Grace's warm sympathy with every enterprise, whether literary or philanthropic, tending to the honour or the welfare of Northumberland, is known and proudly appreciated by all its inhabitants, of whatever rank.

To one therefore, who like Story, had peculiar claims to the distinction of Northumbria's Bard, you liberally extended your patronage, and bestowed upon him, at sundry times, many substantial marks of your Grace's favour. To use his own expression—the patronage of the Great Chief of his native county, was the highest honour to which a Borderer would dream of aspiring. To you he owed the publication, at great expense, of his collected works, in a style of beauty and magnificence, rarely if ever before witnessed in the Provinces; and lastly, to you he owed the "sunset gleam," which brightened and gladdened his last days with hope and comfort.

Neither was Story unworthy of your Grace's regard,—unquestionably his name will descend to posterity associated with the beloved hills and glens of his native county. Besides, his poetic effusions are, though often full of gaiety and passion, remarkably free from any moral taint. His muse was neither licentious nor unprincipled,—on the contrary, she scatters, in noble thoughts and pure sentiments, a sweet perfume over all his poetry, justifying the observation of your Grace: "I hope it may find its way into every Cottage and Farm House in Northumberland."

In this edition, to which you have graciously accorded encouragement and support—thus continuing to his widow, the kindness you evinced to the Poet,—it is intended to carry out, to some extent, the wish of your Grace, by placing before the public, in a cheap and handsome form, some of Story's choicest Lyrics, which cannot fail to exalt the souls and touch the hearts of his countrymen.

I have the honour to be,
My Lord Duke,
Your Grace's most obedient Servant.
JOHN JAMES.

PREFACE.

For upwards of twenty years Story and I were upon most intimate terms of friendship. During the many pleasant seasons spent in his genial society, he from time to time, narrated to me numerous passages of his life, inserted in the following pages. There was in truth, a kind of understanding,—half joke, half earnest—that in case I survived him, the task of being his biographer would devolve upon me; and that perhaps induced him to be more communicative to me relative to his personal history, than otherwise he would have been. Besides he had, at various periods up to the time of his departure from Gargrave, jotted down many autobiographical memoranda, evidently, however, not intended for the public eye. He had also preserved with care, a series of correspondence, extending from the year 1813, to his death; many of the letters being the originals written by himself, of which he had, by some means or other, obtained possession in after years. These original letters, the "outpourings of friendship," are highly interesting, as they indicate the Poet's peculiar frame and texture of mind, modes of thought, and special train of circumstances, at critical periods, either when youth was "purging itself by boiling o'er," or manhood essayed "the steep ascent and slippery way," leading to the Temple of Fame. The numerous letters likewise of his intimate correspondents throw much light on these periods of his life.

From all these varied sources the following Memoir has been drawn, and when the materials were so copious, the main difficulty lay in selection. My aim has been to pourtray, as truly as an undoubted partiality for my lamented friend would allow, the principal events of his course; and more especially what may not inaptly be called his Poetic life. To carry out effectively this primary object, I have, where it seemed eligible, and best exhibited his feelings and sentiments, drawn largely in his own language, from the letters and autobiographical jottings before denoted.

Story died last summer, and owing to long continued domestic affliction and disappointment, had not been able, out of his limited income, to make any provision for his widow. Hence this collection of his Minor Poems has been issued for the purpose of raising a fund for her assistance.

Most grateful and sincere thanks are here tendered to the numerous friends of the late Poet, who have zealously contributed to the success of this Work, and thus conferred a substantial benefit, not soon to be forgotten, on his widow.

I. J.

BRADFORD,
31ST JULY, 1861.

LIFE OF ROBERT STORY.

ENGLAND distinguished as she is alike for arts and arms, with her commerce and civilization encircling the earth, has ever believed that the glorious triumphs of her Poets were the brightest and most unfading gems in her eternal diadem. Beyond all other nations, whether of antiquity or modern times, she has paid the highest honours to, and rewarded the most nobly, her Sons of Song. From the days of Chaucer to Spenser, from Spenser to Pope, and from Pope to Byron and the present time, her Bards have been, with few exceptions, the objects of high distinction. The English Parnassus has, in truth, abounded in rich mines of silver and gold, which have been worked with zeal and success by the dwellers on its green slopes. And its inhabitants have not only reaped wealth from their poetic labours, but honours of all kinds, and from all hands, have been heaped upon them in profusion. Their society has been courted with eagerness by the most distinguished of the land; and so widely has the feeling in their favour spread, that to be a Poet has become a passport to the admiration and reverence of all classes. To the poetic race, beyond all others, Britannia has been indulgent in a high degree, dealing leniently with their faults, cloaking their shortcomings, and treating them, as her spoiled but favourite children, with a tenderness and regard which those eminent in other walks of literature, or in the fields of science, may well envy, but in most cases vainly attempt to obtain.

True, the Calamities of Poets have become a stock theme, but these, in our own land, have arisen, in the main, not from lack of liberal encouragement and sympathy, but from other causes, which need not be discussed in these pages.

Were any example wanted of the encouragement and patronage accorded to poetic merit, it may be found in the life of Robert Story. Born in a humble cot and subject in youth to all the privations of poverty, we see him emerge from the lowly station of the shepherd boy on Lanton hills, the thresher in the barns of Reedsford, and the rustic reaper in the fields of Roddam, to be praised, patronized, and rewarded, by the nobles of the land—by the accomplished Ellesmere, the courtly Wharncliffe, and the Ducal Chief of his native county. To use his own words— Poetry " introduced me to circles where my birth and breeding would, but for it, have excluded me, and it made me hundreds of friends, whose friendship has been repeatedly proved by the most trying of all tests." Not least, it obtained for him a desk at

Somerset House, which if it did not give him wealth, at least afforded him a moderate competency, and allowed him ample leisure to follow his favourite poetic pursuits.

Story was born at Wark, a village lying in the North-West Corner of Northumberland, near the banks of the Tweed, on Sunday, the 17th day of October, 1795. His father, a Northumbrian peasant, married when young, Mary Hooliston, a Scotch servant maid, from the neighbourhood of Lauder, who bore to him nine children, of whom our Poet was the youngest by seven years. She had at his birth almost reached the age of fifty years, and her only other son had grown to manhood. These circumstances exercised a powerful influence on the future life of the Poet. He became his mother's hope, a spoiled child, and hence sprung very many of the troubles and indiscretions of his youth. Throughout life he cherished for her a strong love, and often remembered with emotion, how with aching fingers, she toiled that he might eat of the best she could afford; and how with anxious, and often with brimful eye, she watched until her last breath, his various fortunes.

Owing to the care of his father, he scarcely remembered the time when he could not read easy books. When very young he especially delighted to pore over Solomon's Proverbs, though it must be confessed, without much apparent profit, as he never at any time became distinguished for prudence. When about five or six years of age, his parents, who then resided at Wark Common, sent him to Wark School, where, under the care of Mr. Kinton, he made rapid progress in reading and writing. He became a favourite with this kind gentleman, who well understood the boy's shy and sensitive nature, requiring encouragement rather than coercion to develope its powers.

Whilst he attended Wark School, a great famine spread over England. This terrible visitation, which is still remembered in the north of England by the significant name of "Barley Time," pressed with peculiar severity upon the home of Story's father. His master became bankrupt and fled the country. The creditors seized the stock and grain, and refused to pay the Poet's father a considerable arrear of wages due to him. But such was his uprightness that being intrusted with the care of a large quantity of this grain, he resolutely refused to let his family touch any portion thereof, though they were literally starving. Story mentions the gladness with which he feasted upon even a handful of raw peas.

Soon after his father went to reside at Old Heaton, as servant to Mr. Grey. Within a short distance stands Twizel Castle—a fine Gothic pile surrounded by romantic woods. In his earliest boyhood Story was strongly impressed with the beautiful scenery which abounds in his beloved native county; he was accustomed, at this time, on Sundays, and whenever else he could steal from home, to wander along the banks of the Till. In after life he writes, "Since I became a man I have often admired the rich varied charms of the scenery of Twizel Castle, but the impressions made by these latter views are all dimmed and darkened by the more vivid colouring of my boyish recollections. The splendid Castle—the rugged precipice on which it is erected—the sullen flow of the Till—the ancient Bridge—and the hawthorn glades of 'Our Lady's Close'—still frequently recur to me with the sun of my childhood upon them, and accompanied even by the smell wafted from bud and blossom."

Whilst at Heaton he went to Crookham School, three miles distant, where, owing to the ill-judged severity of the master, he often played truant, spending the day in the woods and fields, and returning home with laggard step in the evening. When he visited the school he usually left his dinner wallet at the cottage of a lame fiddler at Crookham, named Doddy, otherwise George Johnstone. His manner of getting a livelihood for himself and his aged mother was peculiar. The seed time of other people was Doddy's harvest. According to an immemorial custom descending probably from the days of the ancient Minstrels, the gentry and farmers of the Scottish Border were accustomed to entertain at their seed time all the fiddlers who visited them. Doddy, who played the fiddle tolerably with the left hand, regularly as the spring came round, bought an old worn-out horse and set out accompanied by a boy—a fiddler's *callant*, to take care of his horse and carry the fiddle case. At every farmer's house which he enlivened with his tunes, he was paid sixpence in money, or an equivalent in corn; and in his month's wandering he usually returned with a good amount of money, and as much barley and oats as sufficed for the sustenance of himself and his mother throughout a great part of the year. Doddy, by his highly coloured description of his adventures, so excited the mind of Story, that he resolved to accompany him as his page next spring. Upon broaching the project at home, it met with the most determined opposition from his father, who was prosaic enough to consider a fiddler's callant something similar to a beggar's lacquey, and on no account would give his consent. His mother was not so obdurate, as she was anxious that her son should be instructed to play on the violin by so able a performer as Doddy. The lad, however, decided upon the adventure at all hazard; and taking his school satchel one morning went to Crookham by appointment, where he found Doddy ready to start on his journey. Doddy, a long spare fellow, mounted his Rosinante, which was covered with sacks, and behind him rode Story, a chubby lad (no bad miniature Sancho Panza) with the fiddle-case strapped to his back. On the road Doddy gave him instructions for his conduct,—among others never to refuse money or meat when offered; and he would wager his fiddle-stick that the lad would get such a flesh-coat on his back as would make his mother jump for joy when he returned. To Story, who had never been five miles from his father's cottage, the novelties of the journey were exceedingly exciting. When they reached the high grounds, the Cheviots in all their majesty, appeared on the south; the German ocean to the east; and on the north the richly cultivated Merse, shaded with greenwoods, gentlemen's seats, and farm houses, lay like a beautifully coloured map before them. At night fall they halted at the farm house of Lordinglaw. Disencumbering Story of the fiddle-case, Doddy limped away with it to the farm house, leaving his lacquey to take care of the horse. With the assistance of the farmer's daughter, Jessy, a girl of the same age as himself, he soon found provender for the horse, when she invited him "to gang wi' her into the ha' and line his stomach wi' a gude bickerfu' o' sweens'." On repairing to the farmer's hall, he found a long deal table delicately scoured and furnished with the kind of supper mentioned by Jessy. Two capacious dishes filled with rich milk, each of them having a small wooden *divider*, were placed on the table, and around were arranged the master, mistress and servants, besides two or three strangers, (including Doddy) whom hospitality had made guests for the night. After the 'gude' man of Lordinglaw had finished grace, every one was served with a portion of "sweens" or milk, in a wooden vessel, called a *bicker*. After supper the dance commenced in all its glee, and Story relates that he acquitted himself with his partner Jessy, to his own satisfaction. Next day at noon, Doddy and his Squire reached a village on the Tweed, a little to the east of Lesudden, and met there such a variety of characters as could be found no where else. Here was a great gathering, as in a focus, of Doddy's musical brethren, who had arrived from different quarters on the like errand as himself. Their appearance would have formed a capital subject for Wilkie. There was blind Robbie of Coldstream, mounted behind his boy on a horse, which had only the use of three legs; then Jethert Jock, (Jedburgh) astride an ass, which a ragged youngster led by a halter; next, blind Jamie of Wooler, followed by Selkirk Sandy, and Dunse Tam. They were all taken into the farmer's kitchen and regaled with peas broth, which Story and his master gulphed rather than supped, as it was his interest to be first at the next place. In this manner, for about a month, they rambled over the counties of Roxburgh, Selkirk, and Berwick, and were plenteously regaled on the plain fare of the country, including large store of the favourite Scotch devotional feelings. "These, however," he observed, received additional stimuli by communion with the spirit of Watts. The life of a shepherd, too, is favourable to devotion: living amongst the lone hills he seldom sees a human being, save those of his own house; and his occupation is of a nature so little engrossing, that his mind is for the most part at liberty to feed on its own meditations—whether derived from his favourite Bible, or from the eternal hills which every day unfolds to him, and which he contemplates as the workmanship of his unseen but omnipresent Creator. I never yet knew a shepherd who was a bad man! I was at this time a quiet, thoughtful, pious-minded boy; and when wandering on the green hill tops in a starry spring morning, or reclining on a sunny slope of Lanton Hills on a Sunday noon, with the Beaumont winding along beneath me, and Newton Church yard, lying distinct and still, on the farther side, I experienced feelings and aspirations so entirely holy and blissful, as exceed my power of expression to give an adequate idea of them. My poem of 'Beaumont Side,' and sundry passages in 'Guthrum,' owe their foundation to my recollections of those emotions and that scenery." That the life of a shepherd is alike congenial to devotion and poetry, has long been observed. Poetry found Story, not unlike as it did David, feeding his father's sheep on the hills of Bethlehem, and both caught on the mountain side the spirit of poetry. Their situation and their feelings would, whilst following the same occupation, be similar; and it is pleasing to reflect that the compositions of the Shepherd Psalmist were, to some extent, sources of inspiration to Story. He writes thus:—"The Scotch Metrical version of the Psalms of David (I speak it with reverence) divided my veneration with the Hymns of Dr. Watts. I had a pocket edition of it, which I seldom went to the hills without carrying with me, and which I read in the loneliest places, my heart burning with the sweet devotion inspired by the sweet singer of Israel. I was already a poet in heart and imagination, and the scenery amidst which I experienced these raptures, for they were little else, is still hallowed in my recollections." Beaumont Side was indeed the sunniest spot of his early years, and with perhaps the single exception of Roddam, it ever continued the locality on which his fancy most loved to linger.

Let us now go over the ground on which he kept sheep on Beaumont Side, and which, in his "Love and Literature," he has so forcibly described:—

"Observe," he writes: "that bridge whose single arch spans the Beaumont. I once looked on that bridge as a miracle of architecture, and the stream it spans as a very considerable river. Now the river has sunk into a mere burn or beck, and the bridge is rude, paltry, and small. It is called if I remember rightly, Langholm Bridge. I have spent entire days—nay, weeks, about it, running along its battlements, shouting beneath its mouldy echoing arch, or making mimic streams in the channel of the Beaumont, and calling them by the names of the Tweed, Till, and Glen. Let us go down this plain, following the windings of the stream. We are now at THORNINGTON HAUGH. You see that herd of cattle, and here is the herd boy. He is clad in a tattered jacket, his trousers are out at knees, and as for stockings and shoes, why, he would not be encumbered with them for a week's wages,—no, he has to be here, there, and everywhere. He has often to cross the Beaumont—on his own errands, to be sure; but what of that, and he will tell you he'd na' be fashed to be always stripping shoes and stockings to wade; besides, he is cooler and lighter without them. He is just now making himself a cap of rushes,—observe what a grand knot there is at the top, and now he has got it on, with what an air he wears it! He has a rush sword too, depend upon it he is dreaming of battles! See how the buttercups fall before him! "If these were FRENCH, now, what havoc I should make!" His little dog with a ring of white round his neck, and his tail curled conceitedly upon his back, seems as happy as his master. These now are two real friends. The boy would rather that anybody behaved ill to himself than that his dog should receive an injury, and the dog on the other hand loves him with unaffected love, executes his orders with cheerfulness, and receives his reward with gratitude. It would be a treat to see them at dinner, for they dine together. The boy sits him down on a flowery bank, the dog a little below him on the slope, eyes every mouthful with a cunning glance, and jumps up or aside to catch the morsels that are every now and then flung towards him. The bottle of morning milk, creamed at the top, is now finished. A drowsiness comes over him. He throws himself back on the sward and watches the lark that carols over him till he can watch it no longer. He is asleep, and the dog would sleep too, but for the flies which he keeps snapping at. Oh! to be a herd boy again! * * * Do you see that little hill on the south bank of the Beaumont! It is called the THORNY KNOWE. It is now sadly changed. Then it was entirely covered with briers, thorns, and broom in scattered tufts. What a variety and a profusion of bloom did the Spring awaken there; and when the bloom departed and the fruit came, what a feast! The hip and the haw, and even the sulky sloe, as Hogg terms it, were delicious. Many a thorn have I got into my naked feet in gathering those fruits. Mark that deep pool in the stream—that is the very spot where I first practised swimming.

The Beaumont here divides into two streams, which meet again about fifty yards below, forming an island called WILLOW ISLAND, from being covered with that shrub. On this bank, it was that my old father and I sat one Sunday afternoon. He had taken that leisure hour to come from Reedsford, to see me. He talked to me about my duty to my employer; cautioned me against negligence; told me that in being careless in performing my duty I offended the Almighty as well as injured man. "My boy," he said, "you know that there is a God. You see his works around you. These hills were brought forth at his word; the Beaumont first flowed at his command. He made all these flowers to gladden our eyes, and herbs for the use of man. He gives us EVERYTHING here, and if we obey his laws, he will render us happy for ever hereafter."

His father's end now fast approached. Worn out with toil and anxiety, he died when in middle age. On Sunday, the 7th May, 1809, the father, (accompanied by Story) went to Grindon to see his eldest son and brother, who both resided there. The latter had been for some time ill, and to visit him was the chief object of the journey. On that day week the father was a corpse. On Saturday morning he fell ill after a week of severe toil in threshing, assisted by Story, and passing that day and the next night in great agony, expired the following morning, 14th May, 1809, a day the anniversary of which the Poet never allowed to pass without its moments of chastened sorrow. Story often dwelt with pleasure on the character for goodness and uprightness which his father possessed among his neighbours. He loved his children, by whom he was tenderly loved in return; and if any thing disturbed his last moments, it was the circumstance that not one of them was at his bed side; for they all, except Story, resided at a distance, and he had been sent off with the dawn to acquaint his brother and sisters of the impending danger, and before his return all was over. A touching anecdote is related by him of his father. Whilst he lay in his coffin—with flowers strewn over him, a neighbouring farmer's wife gazed on it, and laying her hand on his breast exclaimed, in the presence of a little knot of spectators, "Here lies honest Robin Story."—Praise worth more than most of the *Eloges* of the French Academy!

And now commences what may be termed the second epoch in Story's life—his entrance into the world. The death of his father rendered it imperatively needful that he should take steps for a livelihood. Accordingly, he began to work as a labourer in the fields, but this was a destiny to which his mother was averse, for she conceived that he had received a great education. Having heard that a schoolmaster was wanted at Humbleton, she went thither and took a dwelling and school-house, at a rent of £4 a year; and although little more than fourteen, he commenced schoolmaster in June, 1810. His acquirements were confined to reading, writing, and a partial acquaintance with arithmetic. He wrote a tolerable hand for a boy of fourteen. In the first six months his school became a wonderfully successful speculation. His pupils were young, and under his care made rapid progress in such parts of knowledge as he could communicate to them. Unfortunately, a company of itinerant players visited the neighbouring town of Wooler, and Story took the whole of his scholars to witness their performances.

Fond of display even in these early years, he marched his pupils, numbering some forty or fifty, into the town in procession. After witnessing the performance, a mimic mania seized the whole school, including the youthful master. At first their imitations were confined to the noon hour, but soon their enthusiasm increased, and began to encroach upon the duties of the school. The parents naturally took offence at these disorderly proceedings, and gradually the scholars dwindled away, so that this his first attempt as schoolmaster signally failed.

During his stay at Humbleton, he became acquainted with John Smith, a youth not much older than himself, but distinguished for quickness of parts and knowledge beyond his years. Being the nephew of the principal farmer in the village, he had received a superior education, and improved it by reading. He, too, like Story, wrote poetry, and soon a lasting friendship sprung up between them, which ended only with poor Smith's death. He died a maniac. The lines—" There's a dark hour coming," were suggested by his sad fate, and the elegy—" The Wild Thyme still blossoms on green Homilheugh," is a tribute to his memory. The walks of these two young friends, whom enthusiasm leavened to one soul, were usually upon green Homilheugh, and up where "the moors spread and the rocks are piled."

There they rambled, talking of books and poetry, long after the sun had gone down over the lone Cheviots.

A volume of Scottish poetry, written by Andrew Scott, a labouring man, near Melrose, fell into Story's hands at this period, and its humour and descriptions of country life suiting his taste, he read it so often that he could repeat the whole book by memory, and at last he began to compose imitations of its contents, like as he had in former years copied the style of Watts' Songs. At their evening conferences these imitations were submitted to Smith, whose corrections and criticisms assisted greatly in moulding Story's taste and judgment

He also, when residing at Humbleton, became intimate with his landlord, an eccentric man, whose knowledge, like his library, was extensive but odd, crude and ill arranged. He lent Story books, and in some respects his companionship was advantageous to Story, but in others proved of the most baneful description. This man, strong-minded and self-educated, possessed great powers of conversation and argument, and unfortunately, being a sceptic of the deepest dye, imprinted upon Story's young and plastic mind habits of thinking, not eradicated until his marriage. It must not, however, be conceived that at any period of his life he held, with any decision, loose thoughts on religion. Prone to extremes, he almost daily swayed between fanaticism on the one hand, and doubt on the other, without a settled belief.

Soon after the failure of his school at Humbleton, he removed to the neighbouring village of Akeld, where a kind-hearted person, named Andrew Smaills, allowed him rent-free, the use of part of his house as a school. This act was never forgotten. Whenever Story visited in after life that part of Northumberland, he never failed to call upon this friend, and the mutual good feeling between them only ended with Story's death. He had taught school at Akeld not more than half a year, and mustered a considerable number of scholars, when he was attacked by a violent fever, and compelled to relinquish his school, and return home. The fever left him prostrated in strength, and with all the symptoms of a decline, so that death in his eyes appeared inevitable. Then all his sceptical notions vanished for a time. After several weeks confinement, however, he slowly rallied.

On his recovery he commenced school at a place called Presson Hill. With health the spirit of poetry returned to him, but changed in character. He composed only devotional pieces. He wrote several in the turgid style, in imitation of Hervey; but fortunately, the prose hymns of Mrs. Barbauld caught his attention, and he devoted much time to versifying them. From this exercise he derived the greatest benefit, for he thereby gained a freedom of style and command of imagery, which never afterwards forsook him. When not engaged in school he preferred to walk alone in secluded places, musing on poetic themes:—

> "Ten thousand glorious systems would he build;
> Ten thousand great ideas filled his mind."

The desire of fame at this time, if it did not as a passion commence, grew uncontrollably strong within him. Here are his words, speaking in middle age of this period:—" I remember kneeling on the greensward and praying to God that he would make me a great Poet. Half of that prayer has, I may venture to say, been answered. I am a Poet,—minus the *great*, and that is something."

Afterwards he removed to the pleasant village of Roddam, and there succeeded in obtaining forty or fifty pupils, averaging four shillings each quarter. His evenings were spent in reading, and his conduct on the whole became exemplary. At this juncture he received a letter from a friend, named Mossman, who had been his predecessor at Roddam, and now held a situation as assistant in Warley Academy, near Halifax. He informed Story that he was about to leave Warley, and could get him the appointment. Story accepted the offer without hesitation, and having borrowed two pounds, commenced his journey to Warley, on the 2nd February, 1815, accompanied some distance on the road by his friend Smith. His new master, a pompous and exacting person, soon became dissatisfied with Story, for Mossman had declared that Story could teach Latin, but his knowledge of that language was very limited. Neither did he know much of English grammar, though in three weeks of his stay at Warley, he endeavoured to supply this deficiency by committing to memory Lindley Murray's Syntax. The unfeeling master, notwithstanding his diligence, soon found occasion to quarrel with and dismiss him. This was a terrible blow, and utterly shattered all his hopes and prospects. After remaining a week at Halifax with Mossman, he bent his steps towards home. Observing an advertisement for an assistant in a boarding school at Castleton Lodge, near Leeds, kept by Mr. Sanderson, he applied for the situation and was successful. This was a joyful event, but the pleasure was of short duration. The scholars at Castleton Lodge were of a much superior class to those at Warley, and the rough Northumberland vernacular, and unpolished manners of the new assistant, which had been of great disadvantage to him at the latter place, were now sources of continual ridicule to the pupils. He was so disheartened and dissatisfied that he determined to return home; and in truth a strong home-sickness had already seized him. The desire to see his native hills had been greatly increased by reading Currie's edition of Burns, which he first met with whilst in Yorkshire, and the songs and verses of the Ayrshire Bard, in praise of the glens and streams of the north, touched a chord in his breast of exquisite sensibility.

He determined to be a ploughman, and emulate the fame of Burns; and vanity already whispered the title of 'The Burns of Beaumont Side.'

He left Castleton Lodge on the 21st June, 1815, with the good wishes of the master, with whom, in after life, he was intimate, and walked to Northallerton, intending to perform the whole journey on foot; but on entering that town, his eagerness to reach home became so great that he spent his last money in coach fare to Wooler, and entered his mother's house penniless, but as happy as an escaped slave.

He still desired to be a ploughman, but his services in that capacity were not accepted. Turnip hoeing and hay-making formed his employment until harvest time, when he returned to Roddam and resumed the sickle among his old companions in labour. His wages, two pounds, were of no benefit to him, as he gladly repaid the money he had borrowed for his Yorkshire journey. At the conclusion of harvest, he repaired to Wooler statutes or fair, and stood with a sprig of thorn in his hat, a symbol of the rude service in which he wished in vain to be engaged. None of the farmers liked his appearance, which was about as dissimilar to that of a ploughman, as it had previously been to a sailor. He was therefore, reluctantly compelled to commence again as schoolmaster. The school at Roddam was occupied; but with all his shortcomings he had ever been a favourite with the people of that place, and they encouraged him to commence at Ilderton Moor, in the immediate neighbourhood, where he soon obtained about sixty boys and girls. Here he began a long poem, entitled 'Harvest,' of which Margaret or Maggie Richardson, a fellow reaper in the fields of Roddam, was the heroine. In the following spring he removed to his old school-house at that village, and still continued to labour at his poem of 'Harvest.' Autumn, (1816), again found him reaping in the fields of Roddam, with Peggy by his side! Her ascendancy over him was now doomed to be overthrown, by the superior attractions of Anne Boer, a lady's maid, who had accompanied her mistress from Shropshire, on a visit to General Orde, of Roddam Hall. The departure of his Dulcinea, after a few weeks stay, crushed all his hopes; but the impression she left on his mind was deep and enduring. In less than two years she died of consumption. Several pieces in the following pages were written on this amiable young woman.

Whilst he was mourning the departure of Anne Boer from Roddam, he gained one of his trustiest friends in William Gourley, in many respects an extraordinary man. He had been a ploughman until his twentieth year, when, having a taste for science, he determined to expend the little money he had saved in acquiring sufficient knowledge to fit him for a schoolmaster. On his money being spent, he opened a school at Akeld, and ventured on marriage. Story met him during the honeymoon, and found him studying the use of the globes in a most primitive manner, his apparatus consisting of a large turnip, with a wooden skewer through the middle, to represent the poles, the lines of latitude and longitude being indicated by thread. With such rude means, aided by intense application, he raised himself to a respectable position as a mathematician, and superintended the mathematical department of the Newcastle Magazine, when such men as Atkinson, Riddle, and Woolhouse, contributed to it. The warmth of heart, and manliness of character, native to William Gourley, rendered a correspondence with him of many years duration, one of Story's greatest pleasures. Gourley, for a long period, conducted an endowed school at Morpeth, and died there in 1845.

Before the end of 1816, he had finished his 'Harvest,' and submitted it to some of his literary friends, who praised it extravagantly. The Poem was written in close imitation of Scott's Poetical Romances, which, through the friendship of Smith, he had been enabled to procure. In thus imitating Scott's manner, and applying it to subjects unsuited to it, he committed a grave error, and the Poem had, in consequence, all the air of a parody. This fault he, however, did not perceive; but with all the undiscerning love for a first born, sent it to the press at Berwick-upon-Tweed. The first sheets were received and corrected on the harvest field, in the Autumn of 1817.

XXX.

On the suggestion of Mr. Hall, a Dissenting Minister at Crookham, and a warm admirer of 'Harvest,' which he had seen in manuscript, Story removed in the Autumn of 1817, to a school at West Allardean, to be in the neighbourhood of Mr. Hall, who expressed an excessive fondness for his society. But after he had been at Allardean two months, Mr. Hall obtained for him the more congenial situation of private tutor in the family of Mr. Wilson, an opulent farmer at Camp Hill, at a salary of twenty pounds a year, with board, washing, and lodgings. During his residence at Camp Hill, his Poem was published at half a crown, and about three hundred subscribers were supplied with copies. Notwithstanding numerous defects, there were sufficient indications of high poetical ability scattered through this unpretending little volume; but though Story gained by it much local celebrity, no other reward accrued to him than the gift of twenty-six copies. His stay at Camp Hill was unfortunately of short duration, for some of his pupils having caught the hooping cough, he was rather unceremoniously dismissed, and found himself once more out of a situation and penniless. All the poor tutor's salary had been absorbed in paying tailors' debts, contracted to enable him to fill, what he considered, the high post he had attained.

"Up, son of Cheviot!" he exclaimed, and repaired to Roddam, just as the harvest of 1818 was commencing. Most of his old acquaintances had again gathered together, and they welcomed him to the harvest field with a shout of joy, which compensated him for the loss of the comforts of Camp Hill. He says: "My breast has not since throbbed higher than it throbbed at that shout." His joy was somewhat abated by the thought that his old partner, Maggie Richardson, had died of consumption: "that black eye beaming bright," "that angel motion, sprightly, free," no longer gave a charm to his rustic labour. The verses printed at page 72, were written in remembrance of this graceful "Flower of Calder," as he described her in the poem of 'Harvest.' When the last handful of corn had been cut, and carried amid shouts of 'Kirnie Ho!' he received two pounds for wages, with which he again ungrudgingly discharged a debt.

On finishing his labours in the harvest field, he resumed his school duties at Roddam, lodging as before in the school-house. One of its windows overlooked the gardens of General Orde, who had now a fresh bevy of female servants. One day three or four of these were strolling in the garden, gathering cherries, when one of the handsomest of the girls approached the open window, through which he was gazing at them, and presented to him a branch of fruit. This blooming as it looked, was a fatal gift to both of them, and the source of much misery. An attachment sprung up between them, which resulted in the girl shewing signs of soon becoming a mother. Not long after, he discovered that she had before been in a similar condition, and this, in his eye, formed an insuperable bar to their marriage. Remorse like a ghoul preyed upon his heart; and he determined to fly from a spot where he no longer enjoyed happiness, but on the contrary, hourly feared the vengeance of the parish law. Another circumstance also rendered his stay at Roddam very unpleasant, if not impossible. He had long been disliked by General Orde, and for very good reasons. Story was continually prowling about the General's house and grounds, at all times of night, unless, as was often the case, the house was deserted, and the servants had assembled for a merry-making in the school house, where the dance continued until the approach of morning. On these occasions Story, a tolerable performer on the violin, acted as musician and master of the ceremonies. An altercation he had with the General, ended in an open rupture; and the latter exerted himself with effect to get rid of so troublesome a neighbour. Story, never disposed to submit with meekness to what he considered an attack, resolved to retaliate with a satire on his opponent. There was some difficulty in finding any one to undertake the risk of putting in print this satirical effusion; but, at last, a broken down printer at Morpeth was induced to run the hazard for half a sovereign. Story fiddled at Ilderton Moor for a night to raise the money; and in the Christmas of 1819, the Satire was published, and clandestinely circulated, making a great noise in the neighbourhood. Though a very harmless squib, it certainly was a hit. One of the General's sons laughed heartily on seeing the piece, and remarked :— "The author is a clever fellow. This is my father, every inch."

The General's rage must now be quickly avoided. The school also did not, owing to adverse influences, realize thirty pounds a year, and flight became a stern necessity. Accordingly, on the evening of the 30th of March, 1820, Story set out with a heavy heart from Roddam, the scene of much sorrow and joy to him. The full moon was just rising over the heights of Bewick, as he cast a last look on Roddam. On reaching Newcastle, he copied and sent to the *Tyne Mercury*, a 'Farewell,' beginning :—'The pang of remorse in my heart, the tear of regret in my eye,' and in its whole tone exhibiting the deepest suffering. At first he intended to proceed to London and write for the press; then he indulged a whim of making a pilgrimage to the grave of Anna Boer, in Shropshire, but at last resolved to visit his friend Mossman, who kept a school at Skipton. After remaining a fortnight, and seeing no chance of employment, he had thoughts of expending the small remains of his money in buying a fiddle, and making his way with its help across the country. His Muse had, in fact, as was her wont on departing from a place, taken leave of Craven and its beauties, in the lines, commencing :—'On Skipton's vales and mountains play,' when it was intimated to him that an attentive schoolmaster was wanted at Gargrave, a lovely village, four miles to the west of Skipton, and surrounded by charming scenery. The following is a vivid and faithful description of Gargrave from his pen :—'In the north of England, there is not a sweeter village than the one I have in my eye, and which I shall take the liberty to call Glengowan. It is situated in the very centre of a district remarkable for its romantic beauty, and celebrated on account of the natural curiosities it contains. A bridge, rather elegant for the place, and somewhat large for the stream it bestrides, connects the two parts of the village, which would otherwise be separated by the river. On the south side of the river stands the church, the square and tall steeple of which is seen above the trees that surround the quiet burial ground. Along the north side, the principal part of the village extends : some of the cottages with clean white-washed fronts,—some covered with ivy or other evergreens, and some again with flowering shrubs. A branch of the Queen's highway passes through this part of the village, and thus whilst it detracts something from the seclusion, is the means of making its charms more widely known.'

To Gargrave Story went in the month of April, 1820, with thirteen shillings in his pocket, and opened a school, to which several of the most influential gentlemen of the place afforded encouragement. With his removal to this village, commences what may not inaptly be styled the second great epoch of his life. He resided there for the long period of twenty-three years, there married, there all his children were born, and there he established his fame as a local poet, and wrote some of his best pieces.

For the first year after removing to Gargrave, he suffered many privations, and with the utmost economy was barely enabled to obtain a subsistence. His finances were so low, that even with oatmeal porridge for breakfast, bread and milk for dinner, and the Barmecide supper of roasted potatoes when it could be obtained, his outgoings exceeded his income. The latter for a considerable time only amounted to about five shillings a week, out of which he paid two shillings for lodgings. To add to his difficulties, an order was made against him of five shillings a week, for the maintenance of his illegitimate child; but this exorbitant sum was afterwards reduced by a friendly hand, to two shillings and sixpence a week. Misfortune and privation, however, had a healing effect on Story's distempered mind, and acted like the troubled waters of Bethesda upon the sick. He was steady and attentive to the duties of his school; his fame, as a teacher, spread; the number of his pupils increased, and he began to gain confidence in his position. But during the season of suspense and trial passed through in the first few months of his life at Gargrave, he had often thoughts of leaving a place, where he was only involving himself in debt. Home sickness too, seized him. The great grey hills of Craven had, in his sight, no charms compared with those of Northumberland, which his fancy painted as beautiful as the hills of Beulah. He wrote under these feelings his song:—'O these are not mine own hills.' Whilst in this desponding mood, a friend at Wooler sent him two pounds, and two gentlemen of Gargrave advanced him other two pounds, and thus enabled him to pay his most urgent creditors. He was so overjoyed with this occasion of good luck, that going one day to pay off a debt, he found his eyes suffused with tears.

After the first year at Gargrave, his prospects began to improve wonderfully. Not only had his scholars increased in number, but more liberal terms per quarter were offered by the chief inhabitants, to induce him to remain among them. He soon had the best school in the district, and devoted himself most assiduously to its duties. All his leisure hours were likewise applied by him to the task of improving and extending his own acquirements, which, at this period, were scanty, and scarcely sufficient for his position. Among his pupils, several wished to learn either Latin, French, or Navigation. Many years before, he had as previously noticed, been taught the rudiments of Latin; and whilst at Camp Hill, had acquired sufficient French to enable him to carry on with his friend Smith, a short correspondence in that language. He revived his knowledge of Latin and French by unwearied application at night, and was thereby enabled to teach to his pupils the next day, the lesson just learnt by himself. By means of literal translations, he made himself familiar with the Pastorals of Virgil, a few of Ovid's Metamorphoses, and also gained a little of Cæsar and Sallust. During Story's sea mania, he had gone through Moore's Navigation, but it seems very imperfectly, for he had not retained any accurate knowledge of its contents. His pupil in navigation, a grown up youth of fair abilities, could not be cheated by his master's superficial knowledge; hence Story often sat up half the night to solve the problems next day to be submitted to his pupil. By unremitting attention to his school, he began to prosper, whilst a Grammar school, a short distance from the village, where the children of the better class of inhabitants had been accustomed to receive their education, was shut up for want of scholars; the school-house itself became a ruin, and the endowment a question for the charity commissioners.

On looking over his Poems, which arranged as they are in chronological order, afford a key to his state of mind at various points of life's journey, it will be found that they are in the latter part of 1822, of a more hopeful character. The sanctuary of his heart had long been a void, when he found in Ellen Ellison, a native of Gargrave, and about four years younger than himself, one who happily filled a blank in his existence. They were married on the 17th May, 1823, and a passage in his autobiographical memoranda, saves me the trouble of depicting a character so admirably suited to his temperament. Late in life he thus writes of her:—"I married Ellen Ellison, a beautiful girl, but possessed of more valuable qualities than mere personal beauty, as a faithful love of thirty years has abundantly proved. I have many faults, I can hardly charge her with one, and I say this in all sincerity. We had few real sorrows until we came to London. On my marriage, I was altogether so happy, that I began to think Heaven had forgiven me all my sins. The thought brought gratitude, and gratitude became religion." Hope now returned each day with brighter smiles. His home was a happy one, and he spent his evenings at his own fireside, either in literary pursuits, or in increasing his scholastic attainments, especially in penmanship and mathematics. Among all his labours, and they were incessant at this period, he never entirely forsook poetical composition. Some of these were inserted in the *Newcastle Magazine*, then edited by one of Story's literary friends, Mr. Mitchell, who had previously reviewed in his Magazine, the poem of 'Harvest.'

Soon after his marriage, he increased his income by accepting the office of parish clerk of Gargrave, offered to him by the Rev. Anthony Marsden, the Vicar. The duties of this clerkship were never very agreeable to him, except those connected with Visitation days, and Easter dues, so humourously described in his 'Epistle to Gourley.' To the end of his life, he entertained his friends by reciting, in his own inimitable style, that paragraph, beginning: 'Learn, then, that I am Parish Clerk.' The emoluments from this office brought him in about ten pounds a year, a most important addition to his very limited resources.

In the year 1824, the Poems of John Nicholson, the Airedale Poet, a man of great poetical genius, were attracting much attention in the West-Riding of Yorkshire, especially in Craven, and gained for the Author not only much local celebrity, but also considerable pecuniary reward. Nicholson and Story became acquainted, were often in the company of each other, and the glowing report which the former gave of the success of his poetic labours, stimulated Story's ambition to again appear before the public with a volume of poetry. He, therefore, commenced a poem entitled 'The Hunting in Craven,' in which Lady Margaret Percy, daughter of the Earl of Northumberland, attended by a large retinue of her father's retainers, comes to Craven to enjoy the pleasures of the chace with the Cliffords. Whilst viewing the sublime scenes of Malham Cove, and Gordale, she is introduced to a former lover, who had become an

Outlaw, and inhabited, with his followers, Gennet's Cave, a cavern well known to tourists, lying a few hundred yards from Gordale. Story, in a letter to Gourley, written in 1820, shews the origin of this Poem, and that of 'The Outlaw:'—"I have lately finished reading the History of Craven, and was glad to find myself in a land of romantic associations. All the district was at one time divided between the Cliffords of Skipton Castle, and the Percys of Northumberland. Gargrave formed part of the Percy fee. With me this is no emotionless circumstance, and I already think of doing something with it in a poetic way. Over these vales clothed, I may say, with eternal green—the collected chivalry of Craven and Northumberland, often awakened the echoes of the surrounding mountains in the pursuit of the stag. You have probably seen a romantic poem, of the 16th century, among Prior's Works, entitled:—'The Nut-brown Maid.' I daily perambulate the scenery of it." Another letter written by Story to Gourley, in June, 1825, shews that the writer was engaged on a 'great work'—"I send a piece [in prose or poetry] every, or nearly every month, to the *Newcastle Magazine.* I regularly translate a page of Latin every night, and I continue at intervals my true *Magnum opus*, [i.e. 'The Hunting in Craven,'] and all this besides instructing the young, marrying the adults, and burying people of all ages." Towards the end of the year, materials for the new volume were ready, and early in 1826, the book was published by subscription, under the title of 'Craven Blossoms.' These only included a fragment from 'The Hunting in Craven;' also a fairy tale, called 'Fitz-Harela,' founded upon a Craven legend, and several minor pieces, which had previously appeared in the *Newcastle Magazine*. By the people of Craven this volume, specially dedicated to them, was very favourably received. Only three hundred and fifty-six copies were printed, and the whole impression rapidly disappeared, leaving the Author a net profit of fifteen pounds. In a modest preface he declares—"I am far from having the presumption to claim, or the weakness to expect, a very high place for these trifles. They are *blossoms*, and if a candid examination shall allow that they give promise of future *fruit*, my most extravagant hope will be realized. If on the other hand, they shall be considered as affording no such promise, I shall at once submit to the decision, and retreat to my pristine obscurity,—not, it may be, without a pang, but certainly without complaint or remonstrance." The little unpretending volume received a favourable notice in the provincial newspapers, and also in the *Newcastle Magazine*. A few copies were sent to several of the London literary Journals; but with one exception, the work attracted not even a passing remark. That exception was the *Gentleman's Magazine*, where a caustic review of it appeared, which stung Story to the quick, and forgetting the promised submission to adverse criticism in his preface, he immediately wrote a Satire, with the title—'The Critics and Scribblers of the Day, by a Scribbler.' It had a very limited sale, but accomplished its mission of obtaining for him some attention in the Metropolis, which was his object; but it likewise raised a prejudice against him among the Reviewers, which left its traces long afterwards. Besides, he lost eight pounds by the publication. This loss is bemoaned in a letter to Gourley, in which the poor Poet laments that he must give up writing, or at all events—publishing poetry, and, the misery such a course would entail upon him. He continues—"To many this confession would appear ridiculous. They know not how interwoven, with heart and brain, is the love and practice of song in me. They know not that every sunbeam that glances on the hill, every flower that blooms in the meadow, in short, every thing in nature which has heretofore struck a chord in my bosom, has now become a torment to me, because it continues to supply an impulse which the neglect of the public forbids me to indulge further. I intend, in future, to be merely a schoolmaster."

We have now arrived at the year 1827. His school was flourishing, consisting of fifty scholars, and his annual income, from this source alone, amounted to one hundred pounds! Besides, to his salary as parish clerk, he had added about ten pounds, by accepting from the vicar, the duties of Sunday school teacher.

His position might now be considered a prosperous one. All his debts, whether in Craven or Northumberland, were discharged. His life, though one of toil, was, on the whole, one of happiness. His holidays, or hours for recreation, were rare, except on Saturday, the weekly school-holiday. On that day he 'donned' his best apparel, and usually walked to Skipton in the afternoon on business, sometimes to lay in a stock of stationery, sometimes to read the periodicals, or obtain books from Skipton Subscription Library. His favourite time and place for composition, were whilst strolling on the river side to Skipton, on the Saturday afternoon; and thus were wrought out many of the most beautiful songs in this volume. The happy thought sometimes came suddenly as a stranger, whilst he was musing by the way, and was at once moulded into harmonious verse; at other times the seed had, for a time, been lying fallow in his mind, and on these occasions of inspiration, sprung up to maturity. Occasionally, he amused himself with angling, but though in one of his letters complaints are uttered of the considerable sum some fishing tackle from Kendal had cost him, yet he never became an adept at the sport, because, perhaps, when by the trout-stream-side, his mind was too much engaged in fishing for poetical ideas, to catch any thing but gudgeons. At other times he recreated himself with playing most energetically on the violin, Scotch reels, and other tunes.

Thus happily passed his life. Though his family was rapidly increasing, his means kept pace with his wants. But he had nothing to spare, and could not indulge a strong desire to make a periodical allowance to his aged and infirm mother. To accomplish this wish, he resolved, notwithstanding his former determination to abstain from publishing, to hazard another work, and devote the profits to her use. With characteristic energy, the task of composition was commenced, and soon materials were ready for a volume, called 'The Magic Fountain,' price six shillings. Though this title was given to the volume, it only applied to the first poem, one of a religious character. He observes:—"It truly enough reflected the mental struggles I had endured while in doubt, and the happiness I fancied I had found in faith." The book added both to his fame and his purse. Though some of the London periodicals were severe upon several of the pieces, yet their censures were more than counterbalanced by the praises of his friends. Moreover, it afforded him the true delight of sending a small sum, from time to time, to his mother, which was continued until her death, thus smoothing the path of her last days.

Up to the year 1828, his residence consisted of a mean cottage, but the ability shewn in conducting his school, and the good opinion he had gained from all classes, induced Matthew Wilson, Esquire, of Eshton Hall, the chief land owner of the village, to build for him a commodious house, fitted in every respect for Story's increasing family; and also to enlarge the school-house, so as to afford sufficient room for the large number of Sunday scholars then under his tuition. These buildings were let to Story at a low rent, as a mark of favour. Story removed to his new house in the latter part of 1828, and has (page 101), happily described it in 'The Poet's Home.'

But now all the pleasant gales that wafted him to prosperity changed. For some time previous to the year 1830, the violent agitation on the Reform Question, had reached even the quiet village of Gargrave, and proved a source of woe to Story. So even and monotonous had been his daily course, that probably the greatest subjects of discomposure to him, were literary contests in the *Newcastle Magazine*, where his articles, both in prose and rhyme, were of a severe satirical cast, and provoked retaliation. But now he entered boldly into the stormy arena of politics, and with more characteristic ardour than prudence, violently assailed, both by tongue and pen, the Reform principles then prevalent. Before quitting Northumberland, his political sentiments betrayed at least a strong tinge of Radicalism, but these had been sincerely renounced, and now he avowed himself a Conservative of the deepest dye. Unfortunately for his comfort, the Whig party were greatly in the ascendant at Gargrave, and any thing but tolerant of opposition to their views. One of their chief supporters commenced with Story a series of tavern discussions, in which the latter took so decided and hostile a part, that he raised a rancorous feeling against himself throughout the village, where the people even went so far as to burn him in effigy. These events greatly injured his school and prospects. Henceforward the channel of his life, before quiet and studious, became like one of his well-remembered scenes, the rapids of Linton, where the angry waters of the Wharfe are dashed against a thousand rocks, and form a scene of picturesque tumult. For the next thirteen years of his life, this unfortunate political strife embittered his days, clouded his fortune, and finally compelled him to leave Gargrave.

During the conflict which resulted in the passing of the Reform Bill, he had written many political pieces, which attracted much notice at the time, and gained him no small share of ill-will; but when the King, in November, 1834, made his celebrated speech to the Bishops, Story concluded the day of his own party had arrived, and under the influence of a strong enthusiasm, wrote 'The Isles are awake,' and sent it to the *Standard*. Instantly, the whole Conservative press caught the cry, and re-printing the piece with hearty praise, spread its popularity throughout the kingdom. Pending the election struggle for the representation of South Lancashire, by Lord Francis Egerton, it became an effective electioneering song on his side, and was circulated by thousands. Hitherto the song had been published anonymously, and his Lordship being known as an excellent poet, the composition was attributed to him. With his name, it appeared in the Manchester and other papers, and, thus honoured, it circulated again through the newspaper press. At a dinner given to celebrate the election of his Lordship, the piece was not only sung, but became the text or rallying word of many of the speakers. His Lordship, on rising, after quoting some of the lines, added—"The song has been attributed to me, but, though I should have been proud to be so, I am not the author; and it would be a species of literary theft, not to say so at once." This disclaimer, and the encomiums passed upon the composition, gave it through the press a more extensive celebrity than before. Story now thought that he might, with propriety, avow the authorship; the intelligence was spread by the press, and he found himself, at once, famous. Speedily, 'The Church of our Fathers;' 'The Rock of the Ocean,' and many other lyrics of the same cast, were published by him in the newspaper press. Everywhere hailed as the 'Poet of Conservatism,' he was proud of the title, and threw himself, to use his own words, 'heart and soul into the cause,' thereby increasing the exasperation of his neighbours of the opposite party, and heaping up against himself vengeance for another day.

Having struck, what he thought, a happy vein, and

rapidly brought out in succession the political songs above mentioned, and 'The Ancient Barons,' 'Hurrah for the Blue,' and others of the like class, Story concluded that the time had come when he ought to reap the fruits of his popularity. He issued a prospectus of Lyrical Poems, to be published by subscription. Such was the enthusiasm on his behalf, that a list of more than five hundred names was soon filled, of whom his Conservative and other friends in the neighbourhood of Skipton, numbered two hundred. His partizans in the provincial towns, likewise eagerly canvassed for him. The volume was dedicated, by permission, to Lord Francis Egerton, who also bestowed upon the Poet other substantial marks of favour. In little more than a week, the whole of the first edition had been sold, leaving nearly one hundred pounds profit, so that Story thought himself not only on the highway to fame, but to fortune, and decided at once to bring out a second edition, under the auspices of Mr. Fraser, or some other London publisher. On the arrival of the midsummer holidays, 1836, he proceeded to London by a Hull steamer; but the journey in its primary object, proved fruitless, because Fraser declined to incur the risk of publishing the work on his own account, though he offered to conduct the London sale. Story, therefore, had a second edition struck off at Liverpool, with the name of Fraser on the imprint; but the sale barely paid expenses, notwithstanding the recommendation of the volume in a review from the able pen of Maginn.

Story has left a pleasing account of his trip to London, where, though adding nothing to his gains, he spent twelve happy days, and greatly increased the circle of his literary acquaintance. A letter from his friend Mr. Cronhelm, of Halifax, introduced him to Mr. Hogarth, of the *Morning Chronicle*, at whose house he was much gratified by the conversation of Charles Dickens. He also made the acquaintance of Miller, the basket maker, a poet as he observes, of a high order. In a note book, Story gives a laughable anecdote. On Sunday, July 17th, he went to dine with his friend Thirlwall, a musician of no mean pretensions, who set to music many of Story's songs, and there met Miller. "Three Poets," Story exclaims, "and not one could carve a leg of lamb. Miller tried and mangled it 'worse than ten Monroes.'" After seeing all the great sights of London, (this was his first visit) including a night at Drury Lane, to hear Malibran, and visits to the Houses of Lords and Commons during the sittings, he returned by coach to Gargrave, 'happy to find himself at home again.'

The excitement consequent upon his entrance into the arena of politics, and the time bestowed upon literary pursuits, naturally diverted his attention from school duties. The number of his pupils from these, and other causes, decreased, and being heartily tired of the gin-horse routine of a schoolmaster, he began to look abroad for some more congenial employment. For many years he had nourished the notion that his talents peculiarly fitted him for the post of a newspaper editor, in which capacity he had some little experience. Hearing that an editor was required for the *Carlisle Patriot,* a Conservative paper, he entered into a correspondence with the Proprietary, who invited him to Carlisle on trial. Accordingly, in the midsummer vacation of 1837, he proceeded thither, in time to take part in the severe election contest, which then occurred for the representation of East Cumberland. Sir James Graham being the Conservative candidate, received the strenuous support of the '*Patriot.*' Story wrote several vigorous 'leaders' in his favour, and, at an interview, the Baronet expressed himself well pleased with these articles, and promised to assist him in becoming the permanent editor. Sir James lost the election, and his promises were at once forgotten. Story received, for his services at the election, twenty pounds, and reluctantly returned to his duties of schoolmaster.

These fierce election struggles were quite relished by Story, who eagerly took a prominent part in the exciting contests for the representation of the West Riding, which commenced with the passing of the Reform Bill. Parish clerks, at that time, were held to possess a vote, and his name accordingly stood on the Register of voters; but as he invariably plumped for the Conservative candidate, Mr. Wilson, the Whig magnate, and leader of the district, discovered that the office of parish clerk did not confer the franchise, and caused Story's name to be struck off the Register. Irritated beyond measure at this step, he vowed to possess at all hazards, the right to vote; and consequently out of the profits of his last publication, purchased for eighty pounds, two small huts in Gargrave, not worth half that sum. A relative had, in his possession, one hundred pounds lying unproductive, and offered to lend Story the money to re-build the cottages. Foolishly he accepted the offer, and built, at an expense of one hundred and fifty pounds, three new cottages, which let for sixteen pounds a year. After incurring the usual expenses of mortgages, and reaping no benefit, except the barren one of an elector, the property which in all had cost him two hundred and seventy pounds, finally came to the hammer in 1843, and sold for two hundred and ten pounds to satisfy his creditors.

It will readily be inferred that the wasteful expenditure of his money upon these cottages, brought upon him a series of humiliations and trials, greatly exasperating the difficulties of his trying situation. His necessities now overtook him. He was in extreme want of funds, and turned as usual to his literary stock to see what was available for help. Though 'The Hunting in Craven' had never been completed in the form originally contemplated, he had, from time to time, moulded the whole plot into a drama, called

'The Outlaw,' the greater portion being written in 1835. He now completed this drama, and issued prospectuses to publish it by subscription. The subscription list did not fill as he expected; but the late Miss Currer, the amiable proprietor of Eshton Hall, and a true friend of literary merit, to whom he had dedicated the work, somewhat made up the deficiency by presenting to him twenty pounds. To meet his immediate wants, he likewise raised the sum of ten pounds by the sale of a portion of his library, one of considerable extent, as he had, rather imprudently, indulged a taste for new books. He also received twelve pounds for his year's services as overseer of the poor, which he now filled. Thus he was somewhat relieved, but his anxieties still hung heavily on him. Such, however, was his elasticity of mind, that he was, as yet, neither borne down, nor broken in spirit, by pecuniary difficulties, or the opposition of his political enemies.

It was soon after the publication of 'The Outlaw,' namely, in the midsummer of 1838, that I became acquainted with Story. I remember, with vivid exactness, the circumstances of a meeting at the Albion Hotel, Bradford, where four solicitors, Story, and a brother poet, myself and two others were present. A right merry company was there assembled; the wine and social glee circulated freely; and literary subjects of great interest were discussed. Story constituted the life and soul of the party; his recitations and conversation formed the pleasant condiments of the entertainment. That social party of nine persons, forcibly illustrates the uncertain tenure of life. With one exception, they were in the early bloom of manhood, and all, except two, have long since gone hence. What is more remarkable, the departed were among the most robust and healthy men that could, at that moment, have been picked out of Bradford, whilst the lives of the two still here, were not then apparently worth a couple of years' purchase. Bradford stood at the head of Story's favourite resorts during the school vacations, for there he had more friends than in any other town, and ever received a warm welcome to their homes, or to stay, free of expense, at the hospitable board of Miss Reaney, of the George Hotel. Sometimes he spent these vacations in pleasant strolls over the country; for instance, to Northumberland in 1829, which I believe was the first visit after his run-away in 1820; and once, in the year 1833, to the Lakes of Cumberland, in the congenial company of friends. But most of these vacations were chiefly devoted to composition, or in excursions to the neighbouring towns of Yorkshire and Lancashire, on business connected with his publications.

Gradually the number of his scholars decreased, in proportion as his fame increased, so that it became imperative that he should repair his finances from other sources. From the 7th May, 1839, to the 30th

March in the following year, he wrote the 'leading articles' for the *Sheffield Patriot*, a Conservative paper. Likewise, in the year 1839, he became a candidate for the office of collector of rates of the Gargrave district, at a salary of seventy-five pounds, and in the gift of the Guardians of Skipton Union. Mr. Wilson, the chairman of the Board, opposed him with all his influence, but in vain, the Conservative element being so strong in the Board, that Story was elected by a great majority. His triumph was, unfortunately, both short and dear bought; next morning several pupils were, by means of a secret but powerful influence, withdrawn from his school, under pretence that the discipline practised there was cruel. But whatever the pretext, most effectual means were adopted to ruin him. Now came to pass the prediction of his brother John, delivered in the nervous vernacular of Northumberland, that if he (Story) did not change his coat to suit the political times, it would be torn off his back. The school waned every day; his livelihood was uncertain, and his life unhappy, nor were his circumstances improved by the active part he took in the general election of 1841, when, to his great delight, the Conservative candidates, the Hon. John S. Wortley, and Mr. E. B. Denison, were returned for the West-Riding, and knowing how he had been crushed, they promised to use their influence on his behalf.

Until their good intentions could be realized, a

strong personal effort was required on his part, to extricate himself from the difficulties besetting him. He therefore published, in 1842, a volume, entitled—'Love and Literature,' a miscellany of prose and poetry, price seven shillings and sixpence. Mr. Tasker, Bookseller, Skipton, hung up a prospectus in his shop, and to shew the estimation Story was held in the neighbourhood, one hundred subscribers to the work immediately put down their names. To promote the success of the sale, he gave up school, and commenced a personal canvass in Lancashire and Yorkshire, and obtained other three hundred subscribers. After all, there still remained on his hands, nearly four hundred copies, when he determined to try his native county. Thither he went in July, 1843, and spent some time pleasantly enough with his dear friend Gourley. During his stay in Northumberland, intelligence was conveyed to him by John Coulthurst, Esquire, of Gargrave, that the Hon. John S. Wortley had, through the influence of Sir Robert Peel, obtained for him a post as clerk in the Audit office, with a salary of ninety-three pounds a year, and a prospect of a speedy increase. Leaving abruptly the fascinations of Gourley, and other Northumbrian friends, he rapidly returned to Gargrave, and in a few days started for London, glad to quit, for ever, the irksome toils of a schoolmaster, which had always been, in many respects, uncongenial to his taste, and forced upon him by Fate. Nor was he loath to quit the strong scenes of politics which had so long distracted his mind.

With his settlement in London, begins the fourth great stage in his life's journey. On his removal thither, what bright hopes appeared to him in the pleasing vista of the future! Alas, he knew not the troubles, the funereal sights that awaited him there. At this juncture, one is forcibly reminded of Tasso's striking image, where double-faced Fortune, on the one side, benignly smiles upon her victim; and on the other, darkly frowns, and prepares to hurl her bolts of misfortune. However, to London, on the 17th July, he went in great glee, and with renovated hopes. These were somewhat damped in a few days, when he wrote to his wife at Gargrave, that after searching a day through Westminster, and finding house-rent excessively high, he "feared they would have some difficulty in making both ends meet," and must, for some time, be content to bear the inconvenience of lodgings. In August, he returned to Gargrave, and removed his wife, and seven of his nine children, the youngest only a few months old, together with a portion of furniture, to London, where they arrived on the 21st, taking refuge in unfurnished lodgings, 20, Warwick street, Pimlico, and paying six shillings a week. He and Mrs. Story resolved, by means of thrift and frugality, to fight, to the best advantage, the battle of life.

Once for all, it may be noticed, that his labours at the Audit office, were of a very light nature. He attended at ten o'clock in the morning, and remained there until four in the afternoon, being allowed a short interval for refreshment, about one o'clock. But on receiving the appointment at Somerset House, he laboured under a great delusion, as neither himself nor his friends had the slightest notion that it was not on what is called the *Establishment*. Sometime afterwards, he discovered, to his deep mortification, that his situation was merely one of an extra clerk, liable to be dismissed at a moment's notice, for any or no offence, and not entitled, like the permanent clerks, to a progressive increase of salary, or a superannuation allowance. Nor had he cause for congratulation in the change as to pecuniary circumstances, for after the subtraction of payments, on account of lodgings, fire and candles, there only remained about seventy pounds a year, to feed and clothe nine persons, whilst during the preceding ten years, his average annual income, from one source and another, had exceeded one hundred pounds; besides, provisions were much cheaper in the country. In other respects, his position in London, during the first year, was any thing but agreeable; his country creditors were importunate, and threatened him with hostile proceedings. Placed in this extremity, the Craven Conservatives knowing how severely he had suffered for their cause, promoted a subscription on his behalf, which amounted to fifty-three pounds, fourteen shillings. This seasonable subscription enabled him to surmount a danger, which, at one time, appeared so great as to threaten the security of his appointment at Somerset House. He, at this period, feelingly deplores, in a letter to a brother bard, Mr. Barker, of Wensleydale, the miseries of poverty which now beset him.

The autumn of 1844 brought him, however, joys, which offered some compensation for the grief which had lately encompassed him. Every year, whilst at Somerset House, he enjoyed, usually in September, a month's vacation, and this year he prepared to spend it among the scenes of his youth. The meeting between himself and Gourley, if not as gay as when they and Mitchell, in 1829, were seated over the 'flowing bowl,' was warm and affectionate, though somewhat shaded by the reflection that the latter was suffering from disease of the heart, of which he died the next year. Another friend was absent, his old companion Stobbie, the music master, with whom he had spent at Roddam, and elsewhere, many pleasant, if not profitable hours. This master of song, quirks, and jokes, was silent in the grave!

Hearty were the congratulations of Story's Northumbrian friends, and boundless their hospitality. In their company he revisited Beaumont Side, and many of the other deeply beloved scenes of his boyhood. The sight of Lanton Hill inspired him—and whilst climbing up its steep side, with body 'more fat than bard beseemed,' he composed one of the prettiest of his minor Poems :—' I cam' to the Hill where a boy I had wander'd ;' and no doubt his heart, on that day, did beat high, as he traced it again after a lapse, from the time of keeping sheep on it, of nearly forty years. Though not an ' auld man' as yet, he had passed the meridian, and reached the afternoon of his day, bearing upon him many tokens of a strong struggle with difficulties in 'pushing hard up hill with the cumbrous load of life.' But here on the hill sides of Howdsden and Lanton, and the streams of the Beaumont and Till—he

> Bid the morn of youth
> Rise to new light, and bear afresh the days
> Of innocence, simplicity, and truth ;
> To cares estranged, and manhood's thorny ways.
> What transport to retrace our boyish plays ;
> Our easy bliss when each thing joy supplied ;
> The woods, the mountains, and the warbling maze
> Of the wild brooks.

When viewing, for the first time, since a mere child, the low-thatched cot at Wark, where he was born, or the ruinous school-house, one story high, at Humbleton, where he first 'taught the young idea how to shoot,' his reflections were of a sombre cast, for he felt that the fatal gift of genius had, in alluring him from these spots, bestowed no coveted happiness in return. He felt that in youthful morn his 'dreams of gay castles in the clouds that passed,' were baseless fabrics, which had fed his fancy, but nothing more.

From the lodgings in Warwick street, Story and his family removed to a house in Poole Place, Westminster, and after a twelvemonth's stay, went to Hill street, in the borough, and thence to George's Row, Newington Causeway. This was a fatal locality to Story's family. His son, William, a fine intelligent youth, in the service of an oil and colourman, took fever in the beginning of 1846, and after a short illness, died, to the infinite grief of his father, who lamented his death in the lines, commencing—'My William died in London.' Quickly, the shaft of the 'insatiate archer' struck another of his household, Fanny, about seventeen years of age. These were stunning blows to Story, who loved and valued his children as priceless gems. Grief preyed upon his health; he became subject to stomach complaints, a disorder which he inherited from his mother, and from which at times, especially in the year 1830, he had greatly suffered. He fled with his family from the pestilent abode of St. George's Row, where he had dwelt a year, to a good house, and healthy situation, in Chapman Place, Lambeth. There he remained only a short time, as the premises were required in the formation of a railway, and receiving a small compensation for quitting the house, he next repaired to Church street, Battersea, where, in 1847, he lost, by consumption, his daughter, Mary, aged ten years. A few months after, the family removed to High street, Battersea; but death tracked his steps, and struck his son John, with consumption, at the age of fourteen years. Story next resided in Battersea Square for four years, where he lost, by inflammation of the lungs, Edgar, a promising youth of thirteen years. During the time that he lived in this so-called Square, I spent a Sunday very pleasantly with him at Battersea. Among the objects of his hero-worship, Lord Bolingbroke, who resided here on the banks of the Thames, stood high in his estimation. We strolled through the grounds of his Lordship, and made, owing to Story's undiscerning enthusiasm, a rather laughable pilgrimage to the monument of the noble Author, in Battersea Church. Story, at the time of my visit, was still the warm-hearted social being of old, and retained that cheerfulness and hopefulness of character, which characterized him, though the loss of his children, the expenses of sickness, doctors, and funerals, had left some traces of melancholy on his face and manner. Besides, the pecuniary embarrassments arising from these misfortunes, were not alleviated by the increase of salary, which he had long and anxiously expected. Hope deferred had made his heart sick, as he had, from first setting foot in Somerset House, been induced to believe that his salary would, in a short time, be considerably augmented. Judge, then, his surprise and horror, when he received, about this time, 1848, a notification, that it was intended to reduce the number of extra clerks in the establishment. He drew up a memorial to the Lords of the Treasury, in which he justly represented that both himself, and the political friends whose influence had gained him the appointment, conceived that it was a permanent one, and that it would be an act of cruelty if he and his family were, after his unblamed services for ten years, thrown out of bread and cast friendless upon the desert of London. Fortunately, this petition was backed by some influential friends, otherwise the heartless scheme of the Treasury might have succeeded, whereby one set of public servants, nominated by a Freemantle, would have been thrown out, to make way for those of a Hayter.

Monotonous as his life proved in London, where, for something like seven years, the most important breaks were the sickness and deaths of his beloved children, there are few incidents worth recording. His month's vacation in the autumn, formed a kind of refreshing oasis in the desert of his existence, and was usually spent among his Yorkshire friends. In Craven, hearts and homes ever welcomed him, and such as W. N. Alcock, Esquire, of Gisburn Park, not only cheered him by their smiles, but in times of need, aided him with their purses. The towns of the West-Riding, especially Bradford and Halifax, as well as Manchester, and many others of Lancashire, to my personal knowledge, greeted his presence with pleasure and hearty hospitality.

These journeys, however, notwithstanding the hospitality which awaited him, were the source of much expense; and one of them, made in the autumn of 1848, unusually drained his pocket. On reaching home, he long and earnestly revolved in his mind, the best method of replenishing his purse. For years the old train of thought, the alliance which his fancy had formed between the dearest spots of Northumberland and Craven, had been silently working in his mind, sometimes in one form, and sometimes in another. He now resolved to write a long Poem, something of an Epic, laying the plot as in 'The Outlaw,' in both the districts just mentioned, and choosing for heroes those who figured in the contest between Alfred the Great, and the Danes. At first, he designated this piece 'Aymund the Dane,' but afterwards changed it to 'Guthrum the Dane.' His habits of composition were similar in London to those in Gargrave. He awoke at six in the morning, and having at hand writing materials, employed himself for an hour or so, in jotting down his thoughts. Then on his walk to Somerset House, he mentally composed, verse by verse, whole paragraphs, which his tenacious memory duly retained and polished. Most likely these paragraphs were committed to paper on reaching Somerset House, at the expense of the nation. During the year 1849, the poem of 'Guthrum' was published by subscription. In a prospectus of the Poem, after observing that perhaps from the subject, it might deserve the epithet of National, he proceeds:—"It is the *longest*—some of my friends think it the *best*—I have a presentiment that it will be the *last*." He dedicated it, at my suggestion, to his staunch friend, Miss Reaney, of Bradford, now Mrs. Thornton, who (in this and many other instances) proved that she was a worthy patroness of a worthy poet, by subscribing for eighty copies.

The work was very genially reviewed by the London press, and brought to its author a considerable sum. Three hundred copies were printed at a cost of thirty-six pounds, and most of them were soon sold. From a great number of literary friends, he received flattering commendations of the work, and among others from Peter Cunningham, who, however, gently chided him for copying Scott's manner, and thus, to some extent, detracting from the intrinsic value of the Poem.

Besides the profit arising from the publication of 'Guthrum,' other good fortune befell him in 1852. His salary, as clerk in the Audit office, was raised in the early part of the year, to the sum of about one hundred and ten pounds a year; and now for the first time, during a long and sorrowful period, he began to feel at ease in his pecuniary affairs—and think that Fortune again intended to smile on his path.

But his troubles were not at an end, for this year

was marked by another calamity which came upon his house, in the death, from consumption, of his eldest daughter, Sarah, aged twenty-eight. She had, for some time, been in a lingering state, but Story, hoping for her recovery to the last, was greatly affected by her loss. She was the subject of two poems in this volume; the one beginning—'Fairest of all stars,' exhibits the depths of his sorrow. Some years afterwards he was asked, in my presence, to insert these verses in an album. He complied, whilst the tears trickling down his cheeks, and the trembling hand plainly betokened the deep affection and intense feeling which the recollection of her loss brought to his mind. At her death, he resided in Church street, Battersea, but soon after removed to Albert Cottage, Battersea Park, a pleasant situation, affording him easy opportunities of recreation in the park.

From the sorrow cast around his home, by death, he sought refuge in an autumnal trip to Yorkshire, and accidentally visited the gigantic works of Saltaire, then in the course of erection, near Bradford. His imagination was so struck with their magnitude, that the thoughts so vividly and beautifully expressed in 'The Peerage of Industry' spontaneously occurred to him, and were soon afterwards moulded into verse. On the inauguration of these works, by a grand banquet, where several thousand people sat down, the Earl of Harewood, and a large number of the gentry of the neighbourhood, being guests, these verses were recited amidst immense applause. Mr. Salt, as an expression of the compliment paid to him, presented the Poet with the liberal sum of twenty pounds.

The even tenor of his way in 1854, was not marked by any event worthy of note, except a visit to Paris during the French Exhibition. For a considerable period Captain Hastings, and his wife, a daughter of General Orde, resided at Battersea; and there Story, to whom the lady was slightly known when at Roddam, was introduced to her. The associations of early years naturally inspired mutual regard, and being herself highly-gifted, and a lover of poetry, a friendship peculiarly agreeable to him sprung up between them. Afterwards, Captain Hastings removed to Paris, and invited Story to visit them in the autumn of 1854, and witness the French Exhibition. This sojourn in Paris was of the most delightful character, for with the aid of Captain Hastings' son, the Poet saw, to the best advantage, all the wonders and sights of that gay metropolis, and its neighbourhood. He returned to London full of admiration of the French, and enthusiasm for the Emperor. His obligations to the kind family, under whose roof he had been so well entertained, were acknowledged in some pleasing verses written in his best manner.

For some time past, Story had entertained the

project of publishing a collected edition of his works. Conceiving that it would probably be the last and largest legacy bequeathed by him to the public, he desired, above all things, to connect it, by some enduring tie, with his native county. This object, he concluded, would be best effected by dedicating the work to the Duke of Northumberland, the great Chief of the county. He was, however, perplexed as to the best manner of approaching his Grace, when he remembered that Mr. Dickson, of Alnwick, Clerk of the Peace for Northumberland, had, some years previously, expressed great admiration of his Poems, and would probably promote his views. And upon communicating with him, that gentleman courteously offered his services, and brought several of Story's pieces under the Duke's eye, who instantly perceived their merit, and with the generosity characteristic of his nature, not only gave permission for the volume to be dedicated to him, but suggested that it should be adorned at his expense, in a manner befitting its contents. Accordingly, to arrange for the publication of the work, Story, in the month of August, 1856, took a journey to Northumberland, and spent several days at Alnwick, in the pleasant society of that town. The castle was shown to him by the resident architect, Mr. F. R. Wilson. Story, in a letter to his wife, describes in most glowing terms, the flattering reception accorded to him by the Duke and Duchess. The words of praise and encouragement which they spoke, were more deeply engraven upon his heart than any which were ever addressed to him. On the 28th August, he was invited by her Grace to spend the evening at the castle, where the Duke's piper played, by his Grace's orders, a number of Northumbrian airs. "When the piper was gone," Story writes—"the Duchess did me the honour to say that she should like to hear one of my beautiful Poems recited by myself. I recited 'The Ancient Barons,' which pleased amazingly, and then two or three others, with the same success. Compliments, the most delicate, were bestowed upon me by their Graces, as well as by their friends who had been invited to hear me. On one of them remarking that he greatly preferred the poetry to the piper, I told him he would shortly see these verses produced in the *best style*, from the kindness of the Duke, when his Grace said 'they are in the *best style already*, Mr. Story.' At parting, the Duke said that my Poems would now be read and admired by thousands who never before had seen them; and added that 'The Ancient Barons' should be painted in one of the rooms of the castle, and that he would have it painted in the same spirit as in my Poem. * * I should tell you that the gentry of Alnwick *fête* me every evening; but show Finch this letter, and tell him that I am as humble—and bear my honours as meekly—as any one could wish."

Soon after Story's visit, the work was printed in colours, by Messrs. Pigg, of Newcastle, and in a style of beauty and magnificence which I do not remember to have seen equalled by the provincial press. The designs for the illuminated letters were made in Newcastle, the paper was manufactured in Northumberland, and the book bound in Newcastle, with leather dressed on the Tyne. All the accessories thus accorded with a book which breathed the poetry of Northumbria. The mere expense of adorning the work cost his Grace five hundred pounds—a splendid monument to the Bard of Beaumont Side! One thousand impressions were struck off, at the price, for large copies, of one guinea, and for small ones of ten shillings and sixpence. The work was praised by the press through the length and breadth of the land, for Story had, probably in too liberal a spirit, distributed copies for review with no sparing hand.*

* He received from many eminent men, such as Lord Macaulay, Professor Aytoun, Carlyle, Jerdan, and Gilfillan, gratifying letters, praising the Poems. The letter of Carlyle is so characteristic, that a copy is subjoined:—
"Dear Sir,—I have received your beautiful volume, probably the finest bit of typography that ever came before me; and have looked over it with interest and pleasure—certainly with hearty good-will to the amiable and worthy brother-man who sketches out in that manner his pilgrimage through this confused world, alongside of me. A certain rustic vigour of life, breezy freshness, as of the Cheviot hills; a kindly healthiness of soul breathes every where out of the book. No one that reads it, I should think, but will feel himself the better for its influences. I can honestly wish success to it; and to its author, peace and comfort for the days and years that remain. With many thanks and regards, I remain, yours sincerely, T. CARLYLE."

In the graceful letter of Professor Aytoun, he says: "The purity of thought, and felicity of diction, which characterise many of the pieces, may well excite admiration."

Owing to this and other causes, the profits of the work were not so large as might have been expected, but they were still so considerable, as to add to the enjoyments of his home, and cheer the last days of his existence. Some time in the year 1856, he removed to an airy and respectable street in Battersea, (12, Harley street), where his home was all that he could wish. There I often visited him, and witnessed the quiet comfort of his fire-side. To hear his youngest daughter play Scotch airs on the piano constituted one of the greatest of his enjoyments; and especially when she played 'Bonnie Dundee,' or a Jacobite air, he gave very demonstrative tokens of hearty sympathy.

One of the most gratifying events of his life was the invitation he received from the committee appointed to manage the celebration of Burns' Centenary Festival, at Burns' Cottage, Alloway, on the 25th January, 1859. Readily the Audit board gave him a week's leave of absence to attend this congenial gathering. The dinner, at which nearly one hundred gentlemen were present, was served in the large hall attached to the Cottage. The Rev. P. H. Waddell, of Girvan, took the chair, whilst to Story was assigned as the second place in the demonstration, the 'Croupier's' seat. After an eloquent introductory speech by the chairman, and the usual loyal toasts, Story recited, amidst enthusiastic bursts of applause, his stanzas on the occasion:—'What moves fair Scotland?' Afterwards, he responded to the toast of the 'Poets of England.' He observed that he was not quite sure whether the English Muse acknowledged him, for if she had anything of the jealousy of other females, she must have witnessed many of his flirtations with her Scottish sister. Of the illustrious line of Poets, which began with Chaucer and ended with Wordsworth, he declared himself a devoted, though not perhaps a very discriminating worshipper, being perhaps, in the latter respect, a true Catholic in disregarding the comparative estimates of genius. He held all Poets saints in his calendar, though his devotion was warmer to some than to others, and above all, he held in high esteem the lofty genius of Burns. Some other toasts were responded to by him, in which he paid a high tribute to the Poets of Scotland, and instanced Professor Aytoun as a glorious and worthy successor of Sir Walter Scott. Story's health, as Croupier, was drunk with rapturous applause. During the evening he recited his verses, commencing—'I cam' to the hill,' and prefaced the recitation with a few remarks, in which he stated that when he was affected by any deep feeling he always thought in Scotch. On the 26th, Story was entertained at dinner by the committee and a large party of friends, 'in recognition of his services as Croupier the preceding day, his private worth, and literary merits.' Mr. Waddell again presided, and proposed the health of the guest, in an eulogistic speech, which was frequently applauded, and the toast was, to use the words of a newspaper report, 'felicitously acknowledged.' Thus ended his visit to Ayr, which remained to his last moments, one of his brightest recollections. The kindness and unbounded hospitality of these Ayrshire friends, made a deep impression on his heart, and were referred to with pleasure and gratitude. In a pecuniary light, the journey was not unproductive, for about forty copies of his collected works were subscribed for in Ayr and the neighbourhood.

He renewed his acquaintance with Scotland in the autumn of 1859. Going by steamer from London to Aberdeen, he caught cold by imprudently sleeping on deck, and, as I believe, thus induced or hastened the disease, which eventually proved fatal to him. From Aberdeen he went to Edinburgh, Stirling, Glasgow, and Ayr. At the latter town, a few days were spent most delightfully, with several of his friends. Previous to his departure, an excursion was taken by him, accompanied by an agreeable party, to the famous Glen Ness and Loch Doon. The scenes of the former, viewed in the light of a bright day and merry countenances, inspired him, and he wrote some pretty stanzas on them, which were printed in the Scottish newspapers.

Returning home by way of Alnwick, another treat awaited him. He was invited by Mr. F. R. Wilson, of that town, Architect, to accompany a party on an excursion to the Cheviots, to join a large assembly of the Tyneside and Berwickshire Naturalists' Clubs, the whole comprising some of the most scientific and literary gentlemen in the North of England. With these a most pleasant and instructive season was spent. Breathing his native air, he ascended, with the energy of days of yore, the noted Staindrop, a mountain of loose porphyry stones which seem to have been vomited from the bowels of the earth; and also visited the romantic cataract of Lin, or Linhope spout, where the waters, rushing over a high rock, descend into a most picturesque ravine. The party were afterwards entertained at the hospitable mansion of Ralph Carr, Esquire, of Hedgeley. Story never tired of recounting the pleasant incidents of this day, and as I then resided in London, and saw him very often, I was a willing listener to his narrations. From Alnwick, he repaired to North Shields, where a numerous party of Shields folk, presided over by Dr. Dodd, assembled at the Bedford Arms, to testify their respect and admiration for the bard. The gathering was a Symposium of the most attractive description.

During the whole of the Poet's residence at Battersea, his habits were very uniform, and may be described in a few words. He arose early in the morning, started from home at eight o'clock, and walking through St. James' Park, arrived at Somerset House punctually at ten o'clock; at one o'clock, he resorted for a few minutes to a tavern in the Strand, to partake of some slight refreshment; and when his day's labours were terminated at four o'clock, he returned to Battersea by the steam boat, and reached home about five o'clock, where tea, *a la fourchette,* awaited him. Then, as his fancy dictated, he read or wrote, amused himself with music, walked in the park, or spent the evening in the company of some of his numerous friends in the neighbourhood. With Mr. Finch, a solicitor, possessed of literary taste, he passed many agreeable hours. Occasionally, he remained in London during the evening, and attended the gatherings of the Hotspur society or the Highland society, where he was ever a welcome guest. Often he spent two or three hours with his friend Mr. John Henderson, of 42, Windmill street, Rathbone place, who, from his acquaintance with Campbell the Poet, and other literary celebrities, possessed a fund of anecdote, highly instructive and entertaining to Story.

For the last two or three years of his life, he received, through the kindness of Mr. Williams, the Duke of Northumberland's Agent, an invitation to dine with the Duke's London Tradesmen, in celebration of his Grace's birth-day. This was indeed a red letter day in his calendar, and even surpassed the 'visitation day' of yore, for here, at the Freemason's Tavern, the company was of a high order, and well able to appreciate his poetical merits:—

  Grand day! that sees me costless dine,
  And costless quaff the rosy wine.

lxxv.

Story, on these festive occasions, wrote several pieces, one of which is printed in this volume. Another of them was, I believe, the occasion of a much prized present being made to him. In the latter verses, there is an apt and pleasing allusion to a large gift of wine which the Duke had made to the Caledonian Hospital Ship, which, when a fast sailer, his Grace commanded. The Duke directed that one hundred bottles of excellent sherry should be given to Story. This gave rise to endless pleasant badinage by his numerous acquaintance. Some likened it to the present of sack to Ben Jonson, and stated that Story having been installed as the 'Duke's Laureate,' it was a fitting and customary compliment to send him the Laureate's wine. Unfortunately, he did not live to enjoy the gracious gift, for owing to the severity of the Spring season the wine could not, with safety, be removed from its cellar, and did not reach him until the commencement of his fatal illness. On the arrival of the precious freight, he wrote a letter to Mr. Williams, the Duke's Agent, which, as it was almost the last written by Story, is given below :—

12, Harley Street, Battersea, three o'clock Afternoon,
26th May, 1860.

A thousand thanks, my dear Sir, for your attention! The noble present has arrived. It is cellared; one bottle, however, I reserved; it is now on the table, at least, what is left of it, for my wife, my two daughters, and myself, have each drank a glass to the health of the Duke and Duchess of Northumberland. We all agree that it is delicious: but the THING ITSELF is light in the comparison : it is in the kindness which sent it that the TRUE VALUE lies. I have become quite excited over it ; though I am so ill, that it is with difficulty I can walk across the floor. Still my Surgeon tells me that I am not in the slightest danger, and gives me hopes that a few more days will see me well again. God grant that it may be so! And not to allow my excitement to pass away betwixt hopes and fears, I have now filled the glass to the health and happiness of another warm and true friend of ours. You cannot guess whom? He is the inhabitant of a certain EVELESS Paradise* in St. John's Wood, but otherwise as comfortable as it is possible for a man to be in this world, surrounded by friends that love and respect him, and to be respected by whom is an honour! Now, do you guess? Your health, my dear Williams, and the health of your friends at the same time! I see a smile on the cheek of a certain lady † when she hears or reads this; for she knows that good nature and condescension always go to the heart even of an old Poet, and she knows she occupies a conspicuous place in the portrait gallery of my memory. She and her worthy husband are the two friends with whom I constantly associate you. A health to all!—you see how I run on—all in consequence of the wine! But I must now stop. My physical strength is all but exhausted. When I return to the office, after the present holidays, I will just shew myself to you at Northumberland House, and repeat with how much respect

I am, my dear Sir, yours most truly,
(Signed) ROBERT STORY.

T. Williams, Esq.

And now comes the final catastrophe! For the last two or three years he had not enjoyed his usual robust health. Whilst staying at a friend's house, he had, inadvertently, been put into a damp bed, and had only partially recovered from the effects, when he foolishly exposed himself at night, on the deck of the Aberdeen steamer, which conveyed him to Scotland. Thenceforward he never regained his former

* Mr. Williams is a widower.
† Mrs. George Richards, of 16, Palace Gardens Terrace, Kensington, a cousin of Mr. Williams.

flow of health; but though weakened in constitution, still attended to his official duties as usual. At length, in the month of May, his illness was much exasperated by exposing himself one cold evening on a river steamer, running from Waterloo Bridge to Battersea. With care, the springing disease might even now have been subdued, had he remained quietly at home, in accordance with the leave given to him by the Audit Board. But whilst very ill, and hardly able to move, the recollection occurred that he had promised to engage a public room in Chelsea, for a lecture, by his friend the Rev. Mr. Waddell. In going across Battersea Bridge, to engage the room, the day was cold and raw, and on returning home, he felt as if he had received his death-stroke. Never again did he leave his house. Hearing of his illness whilst in London, I hastened with an esteemed friend of his, and brother Poet, Mr. Edward Collinson,[a] to visit him at Battersea. We found him suffering from bronchitis, and great difficulty of breathing, but cheerful, and expressing a confident opinion that in a few days he should be enabled to return to his duties at the Audit office. We partook of a bottle of the Duke's sherry, which he jokingly observed ought to be a good sailor, as it had made two journeys to the East Indies. Not one of the party conceived that he was labouring under any but a temporary illness, the

[a] Author of "A Tale of Memory", "Education considered in its Importance and General Influence on Society", &c.

severity of which had passed, and that in a few days he would be convalescent. Next day I returned to Yorkshire. He gradually grew weaker, and for a short period before his death, was unable to rise from bed. Strange enough, he hardly ever slept during his last illness. His mind, during the whole of it, was uncommonly active and clear, nay even creative, with a wish to compose, as usual, poetry; but his hand was powerless. From his wife and two daughters, he willingly received unremitting attention. Indeed, the former, at his request, was scarcely ever absent from the bedside during the last days of his life. Till towards the end, the alternations between hope and despair were rapid; sometimes he gladdened himself with the thought that he should, for a short period at least, be spared, and then relapsed into despair—that the inevitable message had arrived. To him, as he observed, how severe the sentence of death, when at last fame appeared to have been achieved, or at least, within sight; and many happy days seemed to beckon him in the future. In his last moments, he 'babbled' of the hills and streams of Yorkshire and Northumberland; and as a final legacy to his Yorkshire friends, exclaimed, (almost the last words he spoke) on receiving a trifling article from that county, "Ah! there's nothing like Yorkshire!" He died of disease of the heart, on the 7th of July, 1860, without pain, perfectly conscious to the last moment; and though reluctant to leave this beautiful world, of which he was so enamoured, his end was eminently one of peace. His hopes of immortality and bliss are fitly expressed in the concluding Poem of this volume, which I believe was the last that emanated from his pen. It may probably, without impropriety, be mentioned that when in the year 1851, I was considered to be in a dying state, he visited me, and then expressed his belief that in the other world we should be conscious of what had passed in this, and that the supreme pleasures of heaven would be something like the antepast which had been vouchsafed to poets in inspired moments.

Though, to use in part the apt words of a contemporary, he might write verses about 'regal Thames,' and speak of 'sleeping at last by that Imperial river;' yet this tone was not in unison with his inmost thoughts. It was not a mere poetic wish, but one entwined with every fibre of his heart to retire on a small pension, and spend his last moments among his 'ain hills'—in comparison with which the hills of Surrey were charmless—and at last sleep in peace in Newton Church-yard, where the yellow broom might wave over his head. But destiny forbade the fulfilment of his strong yearnings. Instead of the 'rural green-church-yard,' he was buried in Brompton Cemetery, on the 11th July, 1860, where it is intended to erect a suitable monument to mark the place of his interment.

In appearance Story was of middle size, and commanding presence. When young he might be considered slim in build, but in later years, inclined to corpulency. His eyes were light blue, and soft in their expression, except when excited whilst reciting poetry, or in animated conversation, when they were exceedingly bright, and beamed with intelligence. Long and curling locks of flaxen hair, which the frost of age had only slightly whitened, fell in abundance over his broad shoulders. The noble brow, and other characteristics of his ingenuous countenance, are sufficiently depicted in the excellent portrait of him, taken when about forty years of age, and engraved by Mr. Geller, expressly for this work.

But who shall successfully depict the strength of affection, and social worth of poor Story? It would unquestionably be a task for an abler hand than mine! That he was a kind husband and a tender father, his widow and three children[*] only too deeply feel in his loss! The numerous friends whose hours he so often gladdened with his fascinating company, attest, with unanimous voice, the geniality of that heart which bound them to it by the most enduring of ties.

In disposition he was exceedingly forgiving. On hearing of General Orde's death, he wrote a letter, nobly expressing deep regret that he had occasioned

---

[*] A son Robert, and two daughters, Esther and Ellen, the latter being eighteen years of age.

that gentleman pain by his inconsiderate conduct. And after his removal to London, meeting Mr. Wilson, of Eshton Hall, with whom the feud was of a grave nature, a mutual reconciliation took place, alike honourable to both.

That he was quick to resent an injury, excessively desirous of fame, and easily flattered, will have been gleaned from the preceding pages. These common failings, even if they deserve the name, were counterbalanced by an entire freedom from that envy which is too often the canker of literary men, and renders them notoriously unjust to each other. Living upon the best of terms with a host of Yorkshire and Lancashire Poets, who admired and esteemed him, his good-will, and appreciation of their genius, were in return, never withheld.

He was exceedingly fond of company, and shone in it, either as an acute debater, or a reciter of poetry. Possessing a tenacious memory, a well modulated and silvery voice, and with scarcely a perceptible note of the Northumbrian accent, his recitations were invariably well received. As an instance of his retentive memory, I remember one afternoon being at a tavern in London, resorted to by gentlemen of the press, in the company of Story and Sam Bamford, when the latter, an excellent reciter, gave a long passage from the 'Lady of the Lake,' in illustration of some subject, and after he had finished, Story, unhesitatingly, took up and recited the continuation of the passage. At one time he could recite nearly the whole of Scott's Poems. Rarely indeed during even a hot dispute, did any violence of temper escape his lips. If he failed to preserve his equanimity, the cause generally arose from the subject of politics, but even here his sentiments had been sobered and modified by age, and accorded with those of the Peelites.

All men are, in their inmost nature, poets; and this alone accounts for the universal delight and interest which poetry imparts to both Peer and Peasant. But though all are so far poets as to *feel* occasionally the true touches of inspiration, and have their hearts deeply stirred by the passions and affections, yet not to many has the Muse imparted the mighty power to adequately *express* even the ordinary emotions of poetry; whilst to very few has she vouchsafed the honour of being her High Priests, and admitted into the inner veil of that everlasting Temple, where each emotion of the heart finds its appropriate altar. Fortunately, for the human race, that portion of poetry which best refines the mind, and touches the soul to fine issues, is the commonest and the easiest understood; and he who truthfully, and in pleasing colours presents it to the multitude, is sure of numerous readers. Hence the popularity of Story's Minor Poems. His Lyre was attuned to the finest heart-strings of mankind—Love, Friendship, Patriotism, and the Domestic affections; and he touched them with the hand of a master, but withal, chastely.

In the poem of 'Harvest,' consisting of two Cantos, with an Introduction, there is, notwithstanding the faults before alluded to, (page xxix,) a faithful and spirited description of the incidents occurring in a northern harvest-field. After describing his lovely harvest-mate, the 'Flower of Calder,' he pourtrays himself in true colours, under the name of Sylvander, and declares that the dear scenes of his youth "attuned his infant mind to song, and gave a joy to after days which poverty could ne'er erase." He likewise paints to the life his companions on the corn rig, and exhibits thus early a knowledge of character both keen and extensive. His love-scenes, with the 'Flower of Calder,' are free from the common poetic sin of affectation, and have all the freshness and charm of rural courtship, whilst the whimsies of the young poet are drawn from his own experience with a faithful and unsparing hand. Animated are the descriptions of the contest for victory between the different sets of reapers, and faithful as all who have witnessed the hot strivings of the harvest field, can testify. But the most spirited and pleasing delineation is that of 'Harvest Home,' the 'Kirn' as it is called, whose festivities are painted in a masterly style, and with a gusto bearing proof that he had often tasted and highly appreciated their pleasures. There are scattered through the Poem numerous passages which cannot fail to please the lover of rural occupations and pastimes; and the whole work, though abounding in faults, both of manner and rhythm, contains abundant evidence of poetic powers, which it only required age and experience to bring to maturity. Along with 'Harvest,' were printed many songs and minor pieces, none of which are of sufficient merit, except 'The Maid of Tweed,' to be inserted in this volume.

His next work 'Craven Blossoms,' may speedily be dismissed. The 'Hunting in Craven,' in the stanza of Scott's poetical Romances, is smooth and harmonious, but fragmentary and unfinished in its plan. Besides, the plot is developed in 'The Outlaw,' of which, indeed, it seems to have been the first rough sketch in rhyme. 'Fitz Harela,' a short poem in blank verse, has little to recommend it. Only three of the short pieces in the 'Craven Blossoms,' were deemed worthy to be included in this volume.

With many readers 'The Fountain, an Allegory,' is a favourite; and certainly it is a pleasing poem, in which the progress of an infidel from error to truth, is described with great spirit and elegance.

'The Outlaw,' a Drama of five acts, in blank verse, though altogether unsuited for the stage, is perhaps the best of Story's larger works. On every page we may discover powerful delineations of character, and on the whole clothed in musical and choice versification. Henry Clifford, 'The Outlaw,' is depicted with a bold and vigorous pencil; Lady Margaret has all the innate grace and modesty which belong to the noblest of her sex; but in Fanny, the Poet appears to have concentrated all his powers to describe the strength and purity of her attachment to Henry. Some of the scenes, after she has been deserted, remind one of Ophelia, in their tenderness. Its liveliness of dialogue, well-developed plot, and truthful pictures of landscape and manners, cannot fail to render it a favourite in the closet, more especially to the dwellers in Craven.

Of all Story's works 'Guthrum' is the most ambitious, and cost him the greatest labour. After a fine Introduction, the poem opens with Aymund, a noble Dane, old and sightless, seated with his grandson upon one of the Northumberland hills, overlooking Bamborough Castle and Lindisfarne. The aged warrior, in high poetic style, recounts the events of the Danish invasion of Northumberland, under the leadership of Guthrum, his kinsman, and the struggle which ensued ending in the defeat of the Danes, by King Alfred. The description of the attack on Lindisfarne Abbey, defended by a band of Saxons, is spirited and well-sustained. During the fight, the building is accidentally set on fire. Aymund rescues from the flames a noble lady, Rowena, and her attendant, Bertha, who were staying at the Abbey. The rescue of these ladies is narrated in the happiest style. Afterwards, their deliverer, wounded, and taken prisoner, is removed to the interior of the country, where he recovers under the care of Bertha, whose charms are limned in choice colours. From her he discovers that gratitude had begot love in the breast of Rowena. Canto third commences with an exquisite description of a morning in spring, as the scene is surveyed from one of the Cheviots. Here the Poet uses his utmost skill to set off in all its beauty the land of his youth. Bertha endeavours to convert him to the Christian faith, and in the difficult task of reasoning in poetry, our author has performed his task well. In the interview between Aymund and Rowena, Story has put forth his utmost powers in picturing her 'matchless form and feature,' and produced a splendid passage. He also describes, with great felicity and minuteness, the patriotic schemes of Alfred, for redeeming the country from barbarism. The visit of Alfred to the camp of Guthrum, is a beautiful specimen of poetic narrative. In the night attack of the Danish by Alfred, Guthrum and Aymund are taken prisoners, and conveyed to the tent of the King, who proposes, upon their becoming Christians, to conclude a perpetual peace; to cede to them Northumberland and East Anglia; and bestow upon Aymund, the hand of Rowena, who proves to be the Monarch's sister. After many mental struggles the offer is accepted by the captives. Throughout the poem are interspersed charming descriptions of the romantic scenery of Northumberland and Craven.

Such are the meagre outlines of this poem. Considerable reading must have been needed to correctly describe the events of the invasion of the Danes, and to delineate correctly their manners and customs. For this purpose Thierry and Mallet seem to have been assiduously consulted.

Story himself considered 'Guthrum' his greatest work, and that upon which the solid basis of his fame would ultimately rest. In this opinion few will coincide. That it is an historical poem of great merit, full of noble and heart-stirring passages, and especially vivid and happy in the descriptions of scenery, will be readily admitted; but the rare felicity of diction, the delicate turns of thought, and the warmth and feeling which distinguish his lyrical pieces, shew unmistakeably where his real strength lay. His first and last essays were lyrical, and like Dryden, his genius late in life burnt clear, so that the last efforts of his pen painfully indicated that the 'living fire' was not exhausted, but glowed brightly till extinguished by death.

Many of Story's Lyrical compositions are destined to descend to posterity. He was essentially a lyrist, and in every description of that class of poetry he excelled. If we look for the pathetic, many choice effusions such as 'Anna's Grave,' 'Fairest of all Stars,' 'My William died in London,' 'We often laughed at Fanny,' present themselves; if we wish for the sportive, what more humourous and gay than the 'Parish Clerk,' and the 'Danish Whistle.' He was especially happy in patriotic and descriptive songs—' The Church of our Fathers,' 'The Ancient Barons,' 'Bring out the old War Flag,' and a host of others, are choice examples of patriotic poesy. 'In May's expansive Ether,' 'Sweet Beaumont Side,' 'Green Homilheugh,' 'Pours the Spring,' may be quoted as beautiful pieces of descriptive poetry. His love songs are so numerous, varied and excellent, that it would be no easy task to select specimens. Again, what more beautiful in sentiment than the piece beginning 'Dear Hudson,' addressed to his friend William Hudson, Solicitor, Bradford, 'The Wives and Mothers of Britain,' 'The Bonnie Pink Flower,' the 'Seasons in Passing,' or 'The Peerage of Industry.' But that which, to my judgment, shews his poetic faculty to the best advantage, in his minor pieces, is the Ode on Burns' Centenary. Here the richness of his imagination, the simplicity of his construction, and the natural turn of his expression, are fully displayed. The Monody on John Nicholson, also exhibits much poetry and feeling.

He wrote a sprightly and idiomatic prose style. Some of the articles in 'Love and Literature,' display much critical acumen, and happiness of illustration. His epistolary style was simple, flowing, and unaffected.

NOTES TO THE 'LIFE.'

PAGE ix.

LIKE Burns, Story shortened his family name by leaving out the letter e. His 'Craven Blossoms,' published in 1826, had the name 'Robert Storey' on the title page; but in the next work he published 'The Magic Fountain,' dedicated to his mother, 'Mary Story, Wooler', his name is altered to 'Story,' as he afterwards spelled it. I believe Story was brought up as a Presbyterian, at least when he was about fifteen years of age he stated that such was his creed.

PAGE xxviii.

When residing at Ilderton Moor, he wrote a vast number of verses. He has most impressively described the difficulties he had to surmount in writing English, in fact, being compelled to translate his thoughts from the Northumberland vernacular to English. By excessive labour and care, he at last attained a good English style, and great wealth of diction. Of this period he thus speaks: "I was happy on Heddon Brae, a few minutes' walk by moonlight or otherwise, brought me 'o'er the moor to Maggie!' and poetry and courtship became the order of the day." With Maggie, he even went to Coldstream, to get married Scotch fashion; but on reaching the place, either one or both repented of the journey.

During the greater part of the time he taught school at Roddam, he lodged in the school-room, where he had a bed made up in a recess. One winter he suffered great privation owing to the severity of the snow storm, which blocked up the roads, and prevented the outside children—and they were nearly all outsiders—getting to school. "Worst of all, my stock of coals failed me, and my pantry was but scantily supplied. When I have come in of a night to my fireless house and cold bed—cold enough, for sometimes there was a heap of snow-drift on the middle of it,—I have actually danced myself into a glow, and then gone to bed, and slept sounder than a king. The snow was piling above me, and the impudent mice running over me by dozens. What cared I!"

Whilst at Roddam, he ran away to sea. Having read 'Falconer's Shipwreck' and other pieces of a similar cast, he had imbibed a poetical predilection for a seafaring life, unconscious of the hardships of such a calling. Following this impulse, he set off, unknown to all his friends, for Berwick-upon-Tweed, with the fixed determination of binding himself as a common sailor, at that port. His appearance was anything but sailor-like. He was somewhat tall, and looked taller than he really was, owing to his slender and pale-faced appearance, a very contrast to his portly ruddy look in after life. The shipowner to whom he applied for employment, could hardly refrain from laughing at the would-be sailor; but told him very civilly that young sailors were not in demand. Hearing, however, that sailors were wanted at Shields, he returned to his mother's, at Humbleton, to get better equipped for the journey. He writes.—"The sensation which my flight to sea, and determination to be a sailor, produced at home, I cannot describe, and shall never forget or forgive myself for; but my resolve was unshaken; and to fit myself for a sailor, I learned a little of navigation from Mr. Richardson, of Wooler. I wrote a 'Farewell' to my mother, my lover, and the Muses. It was a good deal read and copied." Every thing being ready for his departure to Shields, he went to Grindon to bid farewell to his brother, who, however, induced him to give up his project of going to sea, and offered, if he would study the Latin language, to be at the expense. He entered upon this new study, under a teacher, with much ardour; and, in a short poem, promised to give up every pleasure until he had mastered the speech of ancient Rome. But his resolution soon failed; he became negligent, his brother discontented, and they parted mutually dissatisfied, Story returning to Roddam school.

PAGE lxxx.

Notwithstanding the numerous severe trials which Story had encountered, he, at least, thought that his life had in its general tenor, been a happy one. I remember being in his company when a conversation arose on this subject. I contended that undoubtedly he had enjoyed good health, and avoided stern want, but his career had been so much chequered by misfortunes, he had witnessed so much sickness and sorrow in his house, and lost so many of his children, that his course could not have been a happy one. A friend who was present combated this opinion, and on referring to Story, he declared his life had been, on the whole, a happy one. It may be suspected that this enviable state arose from feeling—" My mind to me a kingdom is."

PAGE lxxxviii.

He essayed various kinds of prose composition. A MS. entitled the 'Chronicles of the Swan,' contains a humorous and graphic description of the various characters that assembled in that noted Craven tavern. I have before me the draft of a sermon which he prepared for a Craven clergyman, when he was appointed chaplain to the High Sheriff of Yorkshire, and which was preached before the Judges at York, in the year 1832. The text is from Genesis, chap. xx, verse 11. The subject was well handled, and was plainly an attack upon the revolutionary principles which then prevailed. He shewed that the fear of God is the only effectual check upon the irregular passions of men.

INDEX TO THE POEMS.

	Page.
Anna's Grave	5
An Eye in its Dark-glancing Beauty	24
Ah! will there a Time come	33
Again the Sweetest Season	77
An Englishman's Wife	115
A happy New Year	130
Above the Line of Lamps	136
At Parker's Tomb	151
A Being there is	186
Be Still my Wild Heart	39
Beaumont Side	44
Breathe, Breathe on my Heart	62
Bring out the Old War Flag	174
Burns' Centenary Festival—An Ode	192

	Page.
Dear Hudson	119
Exposed in Life's	26
Fairer than the Fairest Blossom	12
Fairest of all Stars	168
Forgive me, O My Native Hills	184
Guthrum the Dane—Introduction	161
How Sleep the Dead	18
I Love Her	4
I shall never see it more	20
I sought the Halls	25
I have heard of Fair Climes	27
In May's expansive Ether	28
In my Hey-day of Youth	30
I gang frae Thee	43
It is Sweet to Perceive	70
I know thou Lov'st me	83
It is Sad, very Sad	94
It is Sweet on this Fair Bark	98
I saw her in the Violet Time	104

xcii.

	Page.
I was Born in a Cot	111
I blame thee not, World	117
Ingleboro' Cave	120
I would not Pass from Earth	134
It ne'er was Spak'	138
In Youth our Fathers	157

My Love is not Yon Wild Rose	10
Mark, Ellen, how Fair	42
Mute is the Lyre of Ebor	132
Mony Auld Frien's	141
My William	145
My Bark is on the Tyne	152
My Blessing on Yonder Wild Mountains . .	158
My Blessing on Bradford	177

On Skipton's Vales	8
O Love has a favourite Scene	11
O these are not Mine own Hills . . .	15
One April Morn	53
O Woman, Fair Woman	69
O Blest is the Hearth	71
O Lay him by his Father	100
O Faded Leaf	112

	Page.
O Spare the Kind Heart	125
O Sing to me no Modish Tune	129
O Let us be Friendly	142
O Scorn not the Plough	154
Our Nightingale's Fame	178
Our Saxon Fathers	187
Pours the Spring	17
Poor Mary	136
Reply to an Epistle from Mr. Gourley	54
Shake from thee that Rain-drop	40
Stop, O Stop the Passing Bell	89
Sweet Beaumont Side	97
She is falling by Grief	101
She shall not Die	123
Sleep, my Mary	148
She tried to Smile	175
Sebastopol is Low	180
The Heath is Green	1
The Maid of Tweed	2
Though Winter's Chill Breezes	3

	Page.
Thou Fairest Maid	7
To the Northern Breeze	9
The Flower of Malhamdale	13
The Young Poet dying at a distance	21
'Tis not by Day	31
The Wild Thyme still Blossoms	36
The Poet's Home	47
There's a dark Hour Coming	52
Twenty Years Parted	62
The Dead stood by	65
The few Corn-fields	72
The Isles are Awake	85
The Church of our Fathers	86
The Bride is Away	87
The Wives and the Mothers of Britain	90
The Wane of the Day	91
The Ancient Barons	93
The Friends that I Loved	95
The Vows thou hast Spoken	102
The Music of another Spring	103
The Hills of my Birth-place	106
Though almost Twenty Years	108
The Union Workhouse	110
The Rose of the Isles	113
The Day is Gane	128

	Page.
The Bonnie Pink Flower 139	
The Chain is Broken, Father 147	
'Tis Sweet to Escape 150	
The Seasons in Passing 155	
The Peerage of Industry 169	
The Zephyr of May. 182	
That Beautiful Thought . . . . , . 199	

Verses on the Duke of Northumberland's Birth-day . 189

Where, Loved One, is thy Dwelling now . . . 33
Wethercote Cave 79
With Bounding Step 80
We often Laughed at Fanny 143
Who would not be Proud of Old England . . . 160
We rear no War-defying Flag 173

Your Name may be Noble 99
Yon Lass ye see 126
You have heard 171

POEMS.

THE HEATH IS GREEN.

1816.

The heath is green on Roseden Edge,*
    The sweet-brier rose begins to bloom;
While mingle, on its southern ledge,
    The milk-white thorn, and yellow broom.

But heavy snow concealed the heath,
    And loaded every bloomless bough,
When—love's sincerest vows to breathe—
    I met my Fair on yonder brow.

Our troth had passed at noon to meet,
    And there at noon we kindly met;
Our hearts were true, our words were sweet,
    At eve we parted with regret!

I have been blest in rosy bower,
    I have been blest on daisied lea;
But daisied lea, nor rosy bower
    E'er matched that snowy bank to me!

---

* Roseden Edge, the scene of this singular love-meeting, is an eminence between Roddam and Ilderton, the southern slopes of which abut upon Roddam-dean. The young lady—now no longer young!—is still living, but her name must be sacred.

O, love it cheers the hardest lot,
   O, love it soothes the keenest woe,
It makes a palace of a cot,—
   It warms the chill of winter's snow!

THE MAID OF TWEED.

BLITHE I left yon southern river,
   Every glen and painted mead,
Joyous—thinking ne'er to sever—
   Sought the lovely maid of Tweed.
Purest flames of love were burning;
Hope proclaimed the hour returning,
When pleasure should succeed to mourning,
   As I sought the maid of Tweed!

Light the clouds of Eve reposing
   Varied scarce the sky's soft blue;
And the sun, his bright eye closing,
   O'er the land his last beams threw.
High appeared the fair-one's towers,
Green I saw her warbling bowers,
Where had often flown the hours
   As I sung the maid of Tweed.

Still the lofty oak-tree flourished
    Where I'd carved our names before;
These—how oft the thought was cherished!—
    Sadly pleased, she might explore.
All in vain!—Though love's still burning,
And hope would tell of bliss returning,
Pleasure must give place to mourning—
    False the lovely maid of Tweed;

Yet the haunts where we have wandered,
    To my breast are fondly dear;
Where my brightest years I squandered,
    Let me mourn my fate severe!
By the Tweed's translucent river
Pour my song of sorrow ever,
Till from my bosom death shall sever
    The image of the maid of Tweed!

THOUGH WINTER'S CHILL BREEZES.

Though winter's chill breezes have blighted each flower,
And nature is sad in the gloom of the hour,
The blithe smile of summer o'er mountain and plain,
To garden and grove will bring beauty again.

But the Rose that has fallen by Breamish's side,
In the glow of its tints, and the height of its pride,
What dew shall refreshen? what sunbeam restore?
'Tis vanished from earth, and shall grace it no more!

The clouds that envelope the sun in mid course,
That sun yet will vanquish, and shine in his force;
As dark on my soul are the sorrow-clouds met,
But the sun that should chase them, for ever hath set!
Farewell! I must mourn thee, a bright vision gone,
Of beauty that bloomed, and of virtue that shone;
For, though fair among angels, 'tis *thine* to adore,
'Tis *mine*——to behold and to clasp thee, no more!

I LOVE HER!

Talk on! each fault in Mary blame
That hate can think, or envy frame;
Lessen her beauty, taint her fame;
   Whate'er you say, I love her!
I look but on her cheek and eye—
They give her base remarks the lie;
How pure the glance! how fine the dye!
   By all that's fair, I love her!

Arouse my pride: she spurns my prayer
For one—perchance less worth her care:
Her presence melts that pride to air,
   I see her—and I love her!
Describe her weak and unrefined:
She comes—her *tones* the soul can bind!
Her *eye* is eloquence and mind!
   By all that's grand, I love her!

Depress me with the thought that she
Must ne'er my heaven of rapture be:
Blest be her heart, I say, and *free!*
   Repulsed and scorned, I love her!
And while her form—a sunbeam bright—
To Memory's eye shall lend its light,
By levelled Hope's eternal blight!
   By all my woes! I'll love her!

ANNA'S GRAVE.

[In memory of Anna Boer, a fine young woman from Shropshire, who died unmarried. My love for her was the purest I had ever known.]

O LEAVE me here alone with woe,
   And go, my friends, as joys invite,
Where Beauty smiles, and goblets flow;
   Fit scenes for those whose hearts are light.

Another voice than that of glee
   There breathes—through distance long and
     drear—
From Anna's lowly grave to me,
   And it hath all my soul and ear!

Afar in Salop's vale she sleeps—
   There winds of winter wildly blow;
The cold drift circles there, and heaps
   A breast once purer than the snow!

All life and sprightliness, she threw
   A tint of Eden o'er these bowers;
And almost Eden's bliss I knew
   When her bright presence winged the hours.

Our moonlight walks by lawn and vale—
   The soothing words she, parting, spoke—
Away! I must not tell a tale
   My heart can feel, but words would mock.

Then go, my friends, where hearts rejoice,
   And leave me to my musings here—
From Anna's grave there breathes a voice,
   And it hath all my soul and ear!

THOU FAIREST MAID.

1820.

[On Miss H——, a beautiful young lady in Newcastle—long since dead.]

Thou fairest maid that blooms by Tyne,
   Thou fairest maid that blooms by Tyne,
A thousand smiles I can forget—
   But ne'er forget one glance of thine!

How blest the man whose worth shall gain
   Thy young bright eye's approving shine—
Immortal Love shall form his chain,
   And Rapture link his hand to thine!
            Thou fairest maid, &c.

My cup was hallowed by thy touch;
   Proud of thy dark glance, foamed the wine;
And O! its taste to me was such—
   'Twas inspiration all divine!
            Thou fairest maid, &c.

Could all my countless sufferings past
   Return, and in one blast combine,
How gladly would I bear that blast
   To press thy hand, and call thee mine!
            Thou fairest maid, &c.

ON SKIPTON'S VALES.

1820.

[Skipton is the capital of the beautiful district of Craven.]

On Skipton's vales and mountains play
The first red gleams of Morning gay—
O linger yet! ye moments, stay!
   Nor urge my flight from blue-eyed Jessy!

Ye sweetly-opening daisies, filled
With tears from moonlight mists distilled,
The sun will dry your bosoms chilled,
   And ye will smile like blue-eyed Jessy!

No sun, or spring-breeze passing by,
Shall wake my bloom, my tears shall dry;
A desert plant, I'll withered lie
   Unwept, and far from blue-eyed Jessy!

Alas! the moments will not stay—
The sky-lark summons me away!
But while my heart's warm pulses play,
   My heart shall throb for blue-eyed Jessy!

TO THE NORTHERN BREEZE.

1820.

Northern Breeze! that lov'st to hover
    In this vale of constant green,
Tell me, hast thou sported over
    Roddam's every dearer scene?

Hast thou swept the Cheviot mountains,
    Rich with all their rath perfume?
Curled the pure and sprightly fountains,
    Gushing through their bordering bloom?

Hast thou sighed where forest shadows
    O'er the path of lovers fell,
When the hour of gloaming led us—
    Lovers—to the silent dell?

—Fondest of illusive fancies!
    Yet what truth like it can please?
Impotent were necromancy's,
    To *thy* spell, sweet Northern Breeze!

MY LOVE IS NOT YON WILD ROSE.

1820.

[The lady who inspired this, my first Gargrave song, afterwards Mrs. M——, has been dead many years. The infant Aire flows through the village once perfumed by her sweetness.]

My love is not yon wild rose
    That decks the river's bank so green—
My love is not yon wild rose,
    Whose sweetest charms at once are seen.
Her emblem true uncloses
    Its leaves in yonder garden fair—
Worth all the wilding roses
    That e'er a summer strewed by Aire!

The garden rose-bud pearly
    With drops imbibed before the sun
Expands to morning early
    Its folded beauties, one by one;
Each new recess revealing
    A hue more sweet, a tint more fair—
And such is she whom Feeling
    And Taste proclaim the Rose of Aire.

The rose-leaf folded over
    Its gem of gathered dew refined,
Is not a sweeter cover
    Than Myra's form is to her mind!

No dew-gem half so bright is,
  By sunbeam found reposing there,
As Myra's soul of light is—
  My love's the Gem and Rose of Aire.

O! LOVE HAS A FAVOURITE SCENE.

1820.

O! LOVE has a favourite scene for roaming—
It is in the dell where the Aire is foaming;
And love has an hour, of all the dearest—
It is when the star of the west is clearest;
It is when the moon on the wave is yellow;
It is when the wood's last song is mellow;
It is when the breeze, o'er the scene reposing,
Stirs not a flower as its leaves are closing;
And every green bough of the brier thou meetest
Has rose-buds and roses the softest and sweetest!

Come, love! 'tis the scene and the hour for roaming,
The dell is green, and the Aire is foaming
Not purer the light that the west is pouring,
Not purer the gold that the moon is showering,

Not purer the dew on the rose's blossom,—
Than the love, my dear maid, that warms my bosom!
Yet morn will come, when the dew—ascending—
Will leave the dry flower on its stalk depending,
The star the blue west, and the moon the river,
Will quit—but my heart will be thine *for ever!*

FAIRER THAN THE FAIREST BLOSSOM.

1821.

[On Miss H——, of Gargrave, long since dead.]

FAIRER than the fairest blossom
    Opening on the sunny lea!
Torture not a constant bosom,
    Female arts are lost on me.

Shall my love be unrequited?
    Let the sentence then be heard;
And may I be further slighted
    If I beg a second word!

Would thy heart its own retain me?
    Angel charms are thine, my dear;
These enchant me—these enchain me—
    Coyness is but wasted here.

Cloud and gleam, by turns that fly, love,
    Mark a Craven's summer day—
Be not thou a changeful sky, love;
    Let thy smile for ever play!

Flowers that in the shade would perish,
    In the light will blossom high;
And my love will only flourish
    In the sunshine of thine eye!

THE FLOWER OF MALHAMDALE.

1821.

[This lady was a Miss Dewhurst, who died at Airton in Malhamdale, in, I think, her 16th year.]

If on some bright and breezeless eve,
    When falls the ripe rose leaf by leaf,
The moralising bard will heave
    A sigh that seems allied to grief,—

Shall I be blithe, shall I be mute,
    Nor shed the tear, nor pour the wail,
When death has blighted to its root
    The sweetest Flower of Malhamdale?

Her form was like the fair sun-stream
    That glances through the mists of noon—
Ah! little thought we that its beam
    Would vanish from our glens so soon!
Yet when her eye had most of mirth,
    And when her cheek the least was pale,
They talked of purer worlds than earth—
    She could not stay in Malhamdale!

The placid depth of that dark eye,
    The wild-rose tint of that fair cheek—
Will still awake the long-drawn sigh,
    While Memory of the past shall speak.
And we can never be but pained
    To think, when gazing on that vale,
One Angel more to Heaven is gained,
    But one is lost to Malhamdale!

I may not tell what dreams were mine—
    Dreams laid in bright futurity—
When the full, soft, and partial shine
    Of that fair eye was turned on me.

Enough, enough—the blooming wreath
  Of Love, and Hope, and Joy, is pale,
And now its withering perfumes breathe
  O'er yon new grave in Malhamdale!

O THESE ARE NOT MINE OWN HILLS.

1821.

[On arriving in Craven, whither I had come on foot, and seeing the hills—so like, and yet so unlike the Northumbrian mountains—I became seized with a HOME SICKNESS the most intense. I fancied myself banished to a far-distant land; and if the reader, who may be inclined to smile at the idea, will reflect that railways then were not; that stage coaches were above my means; and that my estimate of distance was founded on my power as a pedestrian; he will see that the idea was not so very absurd.]

O THESE are not mine own hills,
  Fair though their verdure be;
Distant far mine own hills,
  That used to look so kind on me!
These may have their rock and cairn,
  Their blooming heath, and waving fern—
But O! they stand so strange and stern,
  And never seem like friends to me.

"Where, pr'ythee, rise thine own hills?
　　In France or brighter Italy?
What fruit is on thine own hills,
　　That we must deem so fair to see?
Grows in Summer's constant shine,
The orange there, or purpling vine?
Does myrtle with the rose entwine
　　On mountains so beloved by thee?"

All bleak along mine own hills
　　The heather waves, the bracken free;
The fruit upon mine own hills
　　Is scarlet hip and blaeberry.
And yet I would not them exchange,
'Mid gay Italian scenes to range;
No! vine-clad hills would look as strange,
　　As stern, and lone, as *these* to me!

In boyhood, on mine own hills,
　　I plucked the flower, and chased the bee;
In youth, upon mine own hills,
　　I wooed my loves by rock and tree:
'Tis hence my love—to tears—they claim;
And let who will the weakness blame,
But when, in sleep, I dream of them—
　　I would not wake aught else to see!

POURS THE SPRING.

1821.

[Howdsden—which I have softened into Howsden—a beautiful hill overlooking the Beaumont. It is remarkable as being always the very first to acknowledge, by its verdure, the favours of returning Spring. Its base, when I kept sheep upon it in my boyish days, used to exhibit a perfect forest of broom.]

Pours the Spring its earliest green
    Upon Howsden still?
Are the milk-white hawthorns seen
    Upon Howsden still?
Does the tall and grove-like broom,
With its moist and yellow bloom,
Shed a glory and perfume
    Upon Howsden still?

Rests the white and downy cloud
    Upon Howsden still?
Is the skylark's carol loud
    Upon Howsden still?
Is the curlew seldom dumb?
And the wild bees—do they come,
As of old to sip and hum
    Upon Howsden still?

Sits the happy shepherd boy
    Upon Howsden still,
Singing blithe his song of joy
    Upon Howsden still?
While far beneath his eyes
The blue stream of Beaumont lies,
And her liquid murmurs rise
    Upon Howsden still?

Ah! the Summer sheds delight
    Upon Howsden still;
And I walk, in dreams by night,
    Upon Howsden still?
When waking 'mid my joy,
I but meet the world's annoy,
And wish I were a boy
    Upon Howsden still!

HOW SLEEP THE DEAD.

1821.

How sleep the dead in yon church yard,
    Where chequering moonbeams purely fall?
How sleep the dead beneath the sward?
    Calmly—softly—sweetly all!

In mute companionship they lie—
    No hearts that ache, no eyes that weep!
Pain, sickness, trouble, come not nigh
    The beds of those that yonder sleep.

Around, the world is passion-tost—
    War, murder, crime, for ever reign;
Of sacred peace alone may boast
    The church-yard's undisturbed domain.

The stormy sea of human life,
    With all its surges, roars around;
Their barrier-wall repels its strife—
    No wave breaks o'er their hallowed ground!

Around, the summer sun may scorch—
    The dead feel not the sultry ray;
Winter may howl in spire and porch—
    The dead are reckless of his sway.

Thus sleep the dead in yon church yard,
    Where chequering moonbeams purely fall;
Thus sleep the dead beneath the sward—
    Calmly—softly—sweetly all!

I SHALL NEVER SEE IT MORE.

1821.

I shall never see it more! save in visions during sleep,
When—but half deceived—I gaze on it, and as I gaze I weep;
But 'tis blossomed bright in Memory yet, and shades the verdant steep,
    The sweetest hawthorn tree on the banks of the Till!

'Twas a lovely eve in Spring, and the crimson of the west
Lay like a dream of heaven on the river's gentle breast,
When we met beside the hawthorn tree, in milk-white blossoms dressed,
    The loving and the loved, on the banks of the Till!

I have wandered—wandered long in the heartless ways of men,
And have often felt the thrill of love—but never more as then,
When we lay in young love's happy trance amid the silent glen—
    Beside the hawthorn tree on the banks of the Till!

My Mary was as pure as the bloom upon the tree!
  She died—and left my heart exposed to vice and
    misery;
She drank of life's first rapture-cup, and what is left
    to me,
  But a worthless draught, afar from the banks of the
    Till!

THE YOUNG POET DYING AT A DISTANCE FROM HOME.

1821.

(Written during a slight attack of illness. I imagined I was going to die—far from Roddam-dean, where, in my feverish excitement, I wished to be buried.)

O BURY me not in yon strange spot of earth!
  My rest never sweet, never tranquil can be;
But bear me away to the land of my birth,
  To a scene—O how dear, and how pleasant to me!
If you saw how the sunbeams illumine the mountains,
  How brightly they lie in the glen that I choose—

Could the song of its birds, and the gush of its foun-
    tains,
  Through *your* souls the rapture and freshness diffuse
Which in life's happy morning they shed over *mine*—
O! your hearts would confess it is all but divine!

Nay, call it not raving! A stranger I came,
  And a stranger amongst you I ever have been:
When I stepped from my circle, you found me the
    same
  Vain trifler as thousands beside in the scene.
But I lived in a circle of fancy and feeling,
  A world of fair forms, a creation of bliss,
Though never to you the dear secret revealing:
  My first and my latest disclosure is this,
This dying request—the last night of the dream!—
O! do not despise it, though wild it may seem.

I know it—the grave which to me you assign,
  Is black in the shade of your dreary church-wall,
Where nettle and hemlock their rankness combine,
  And the worm and sullen toad loathsomely crawl.
O! where is the primrose, so meet for adorning
  The grave of a Minstrel cut off in his bloom?
O! where is the daisy, to shed in the morning
  The tears it had gathered by night, for my doom?
And dearer—O! dearer than anguish can tell,
Where, where are the friends that have loved me so
    well?

Thrice blest be those tears! they descend on my heart
    Like the soft rain of Spring on a perishing flower;
And may I expire in the hope they impart,
    That—yet—I shall rest by my favourite bower?
Heaven love you for that! Like the flower I have shown you,
    No more to expand in the loveliest ray,
And breathing its last sigh of perfume upon you,
    My spirit, all grateful, shall vanish away!
For laid in the glen, by the stream and the tree,
Deep, hallowed, and happy, my slumber shall be!

See! one aged Mourner comes, trembling, to place
    A weak, withered hand on the grave of her son—
See! Friendship, to tell how I strove in the race,
    But died ere the chaplet of glory was won—
And Beauty—I plaited a wreath for that Maiden
    When warm was my heart, and my fancy was high;
See! Beauty approaches with summer-flowers laden,
    And strews them when nought but the blackbird is nigh!
Thus, thus shall I rest, with a charm on my name,
In the shower-mingled sunshine of Love and of Fame!

AN EYE IN ITS DARK-GLANCING BEAUTY.

[On Miss H——, already alluded to. See ANTE.]

An eye in its dark-glancing beauty hath spoken,
    A lip hath been pressed like a rose-bud in dew,
And the clasp of a soft hand has thrilled as a token
    Through fibre and vein—that my Fanny is true!

There's a tint of romance in the sunbeam that lightens
    By turns the green vale, and the mountain's wild hue;
It comes from the thought that internally brightens,
    The heart-blessing thought—that my Fanny is true!

There's a voice in the gale, as it sighingly wanders
    Where the young buds of Spring open green on the view;
There's a voice in the stream, as it purely meanders,
    Breathing fresh o'er the soul—that my Fanny is true!

The lark as he soars from the strained eye of wonder,
    Or brushes the white cloud that streaks the fine blue,
Sends down his loud note to the choristers under,
    And wood and vale ring with—my Fanny is true!

O soften, my song! for a transport is given,
  To which the best chords of the bosom are due;
And sing like the gale on a rose-bank at even,
  In a long sigh of bliss—that my Fanny is true!

I SOUGHT THE HALLS.

1822.

[The halls meant were those of Eshton, where Ellen Ellison—now Mrs. Story—had resided. Set to music by Godby.]

I sought the halls, sweet Ellen,
  Where thou wast wont to be;
And I deemed, my dearest Ellen,
  They still were bright with thee.
As sun-hues linger on the hill
  Long after evening falls,
So seemed the light of beauty still
  To gild the lonely halls!

I sought the garden, Ellen,
  I sought the arbour fair;
And I vow my dearest Ellen,
  Thy sweetness met me there.

The brightest Rose had left the bower,
But still her favourite scene
Retained the fragrance of the flower,
And told where she had been!

EXPOSED IN LIFE'S.

1822.

On the same.

Exposed in life's neglected vale,
To scorch in sun, or waste in gale,
The wild-rose tints so softly pale
　　That first attracted me, love—
O unbefriended! take my aid,
Accept my shelter and my shade,
Where suns shall but in gleams pervade,
　　And storms blow calm to thee, love!

The summer leaves of Fortune now
Have clothed my every spreading bough;
One ornament I want, and thou—
　　O thou art that to me, love;

Then come—and, by my hopes refined!
No Oak that ever braved the wind,
So screened the Woodbine round him twined,
As I will shelter thee, love!

I HAVE HEARD OF FAIR CLIMES.

1822.

[The home-sickness begins to disappear.]

I HAVE heard of fair climes lying nearer the sun,
Where the summer and autumn are blent into one,
Where the flowers in unfailing succession come forth,
And brighter of hue than the flowers of the north,
Where the fruit and the blossom adorn the same tree—
Yet Craven, green Craven, 's the land for me.

I have heard of the azure enchanting all eyes,
The deep, cloudless blue of Italian skies—
But give me the wild heaven, now gloomy, now gay,
That with shadow and sunshine still varies the day,
Forming scenes which a painter or bard loves to see—
And Craven, green Craven, 's the land for me!

Can lands where the summer and autumn entwine,
Exhibit a contrast more pleasing than thine?
Spring smiles in yon vale where the river is rolled,
And Autumn has hung yonder mountain with gold;
Yon beech tree stands red on an emerald lea—
O, Craven, green Craven, 's the land for me!

Why talk of Circassia as Beauty's domain?
Or why of the dark-glancing daughters of Spain?
We have maids that might realise dreams of above,
Too lovely—if aught were too lovely—for love,
As sweet as their Spring, as their mountain-winds free—
Yes! Craven, green Craven, 's the land for me!

IN MAY'S EXPANSIVE ETHER.

1823.

[On Ellen Ellison.]

In May's expansive ether
   Floats many a downy cloud—
Some white and pure as silver,
   Some edged and streaked wi' gowd.

I care na for the gorgeous sight,
   Though fair as sight may be;
My bonnie Craven lassie
   Is the dearest sight to me!

All yellow as the cloudlet,
   My love's bright locks are laid,
And radiant as its silver
   The neck and brow they shade.
The heart that beats within her breast
   Is now na langer free—
My bonnie Craven lassie
   Has bestowed her heart on me!

The bloom is on the hawthorn,
   The green leaf's on the tree,
The king-cup gems the meadow,
   And the gowan stars the lea.
I care na for the charms o' spring,
   Though fair those charms may be—
My bonnie Craven lassie
   Is the dearest charm to me!

On yonder bank a blossom
   Is mirrored in the lake—
The next wild breeze that sweeps it
   The shadowy charm will break.

But what wild breeze shall e'er efface
  The impress *here* of thee?
My bonnie Craven lassie
  Thou art wealth and fame to me!

IN MY HEY-DAY OF YOUTH.

1823.

In my hey-day of youth, when each pulse beat to glee,
I roved amang lasses o' ilka degree,
The gentle, the semple, the cauld, and the kind,
The neat country girl, and the lady refined;
But when I looked out a companion for life,
I found nane to suit like my ain little Wife!

She was heir to na wealth, but to balance it a',
Her tastes were na nice, and her wishes were la';
Her forbears were poor, but to tell it I'm fain,
She need na to blush for their deeds nor her ain;
The tap o' the cassay they trod on thro' life,
And left their fair fame to my ain little Wife!

By the ingle at e'en, when my labour is o'er,
I draw my chair ben on a nice sanded floor,
Then I tell her a tale, or she sings me a sang,
And the lang winter nights are to us never lang,
While to keep a' things tidy 's the pride o' her life,
And I ca' her in rapture my ain little Wife!

If there's gloom in her e'e—as a vapour will rise
And darken the bluest o' Simmer' blue skies—
It stays na sae lang till it quite disappears,
Laughed aff by a love-blink, or melted in tears,
In tears that bring feelings the sweetest in life,
As I clasp to my bosom my ain little Wife!

'TIS NOT BY DAY.

1824.

'Tis not by day, however bright
  The beauty of the day may be,
'Tis in the night, 'tis in the night,
  My holiest musings dwell on Thee!

'Tis true, thy glorious hand I view
　　In every leaf that greens the tree;
And not a floweret blooms in dew,
　　But wakes some lovely thought of Thee!

'Tis true the mountain soaring high,
　　The river rolling to the sea,
The blue and boundless stretch of sky—
　　Bid the awed spirit turn to Thee.

But few and brief such feelings are;
　　From business and from day they flee;
Ten thousand nameless chances jar
　　On bosom-chords, though tuned to Thee.

'Tis in the night, when nought around
　　The ear can hear, the eye can see;
When all seems laid in sleep profound,
　　Except my watching Soul and Thee;

'Tis then, my God! I feel thy power
　　And love, from all distraction free!
My couch is Heaven in that high hour!
　　Thou'rt round me—I am wrapped in Thee!

WHERE, LOVED ONE! IS THY DWELLING NOW?

1824.

[In memory of Miss Sarah Johnson, a fair pupil of mine, who died in her thirteenth year. She was the daughter of the late Thomas Johnson, Esq., of Eshton.]

WHERE, loved One! is thy dwelling now?
   In scenes where thou wert wont to be,
Thy laughing eye, thy open brow,
   Thy sylph-like form no more we see.
There's grief around thy father's hearth,
Which time shall scarcely change to mirth!

There's weeping in thy father's hall—
   Its chambers, which so lately rung
To thy light step or lively call,
   Seem dark as if with sable hung.
Too well their gloom declares that thou
Hast left thy father's dwelling now!

When last I looked upon thy face,
   Thy fair cheek wore a pallid hue;
Yet kept thine eye its wonted grace,
   And wildly free thy dark hair flew.

I little thought *whose* breath had passed
Across thy features like a blast——

I little thought that Death had blown
    E'en then his sickening breath on thee!
I little thought thy glance and tone
    Then spoke and beamed their last for me!
My parting word unthinking fell—
I dreamt not of a *last* farewell!

But the same Moon, whose crescent beam
    Beheld thee in accustomed bloom,
Was seen to pour her waning stream
    Of dewy radiance round thy tomb:
O loveliest and loved One, thou
Hast found a darksome dwelling now!

I went to where thy grave was scooped—
    There children, seeming half to grieve,
Stood round, in gazing clusters grouped;
    I saw it, and could scarce believe
So dark and damp a cell could be
For aught so light and gay as thee!

Yet so it was. I saw thee lowered,
    And heard upon thy coffin-lid
With heavy sound the dull earth showered,
    Till dust by dust was heaped and hid;

And looks I marked whose anguish said
Life's highest charm with thee was dead!

Then fled our frailest and our last
    Illusion—that in which we think,
While ours the dust whence life has passed,
    There still is *one* unshivered link.
That the grave broke; and all of thee
Hath faded to a *memory!*

There was a time when "in thy mirth"
    Thou archly "bad'st me write on thee;"
And now, lost flower of fairest birth,
    "I write—what thou shalt never see!"
Alas, how sad a song hath paid
Request scarce thought, and lightly made!

But shall my song have mournful close?
    O! not for *thee* our tears should fall;
Thou art where Spring eternal blows—
    Thou art where God is all in all!
Thine claim our grief; but, loved One! *thou*
Hast found a glorious dwelling now!

THE WILD THYME STILL BLOSSOMS.

1824.

[Homil-heugh is the name of one of the Cheviot Hills, in the vicinity of Wooler. At the foot of this mountain was fought the celebrated battle in which Hotspur took Archibald, Earl of Douglas, and many others of the Scottish nobility prisoners. The ultimate consequences of that conflict to the House of Percy, are familiar to every reader of English history and of Shakspeare. The mountain is endeared to me by recollections of a thousand wanderings about it, in company with the subject of this lyric—John Smith, of Humbleton—the most beloved, as he was the first, of my youthful friends.]

The wild thyme still blossoms on green Homil-heugh,
    The daisy and crow-flower mingle there still;
And the young, as in other years, climb it to view
    The wanderings bright of the Glen and the Till.
But where—where is He who delighted to view
The charms of that valley from green Homil-heugh.

O Memory! I need not invoke thee to roll
    Away the dark mists of long years, and to bring
The light of that time on my sorrowing soul,
    When together we roved in our Manhood's gay spring;
Too often, for happiness, pass in review
The days we have spent upon green Homil-heugh!

How we talked! as we loitered by dell or by shelf,
    Or sat on some moss-covered crag in the sun—
We spoke not of station, we spoke not of pelf,
    We talked but of Bards and the Glory they won :
And bright were the hopes—ah, to *both* how untrue!—
Our young bosoms cherished on green Homil-heugh.

O! who could have thought, that beheld the fair dawn—
    Beheld of his Mind the first splendour unfurled—
That a dark cloud would o'er it so shortly be drawn,
    And its light be for ever eclipsed to the world?
That the harp whose wild strains he so daringly threw
So soon would be silent on green Homil-heugh?

But 'tis so with all bright things.   The rose newly blown
    Soon withers; the Sunbeam is quenched in the shower;
The Rainbow just shines on the cloud, and is gone;
    The Lightning just flashes, and past is its power.
And the soul of my first friend hath vanished like dew
From the calm morning side of the green Homil-heugh!

AH! WILL THERE A TIME COME.

1824.

Ah! will there a time come, when coldly above me
  The earth of the valley I tread shall be laid;
When the tears of the few that now cling to and love
    me,
Unheeded shall fall—like the dew in the shade?

When each charm, and each change, and each scene
    it delights me
  To note and remember, to me shall be o'er;
When all that to song or to musing invites me,
  To musing or song shall invite me no more?

When rainbows o'er green, gleaming landscapes shall
    brighten,
  And melody warble from grove and from sky;
When tempests shall howl, or grim thunder-clouds
    lighten,
  And my breast give no throb, and no sparkle my
    eye?

When Springs shall refreshen the hues of the mountain,
    And Summers be-gem with young blossoms the lea;
And Autumns with red leaves bestrew the chill fountain,
    And white Winters dazzle—unwitnessed by me?

So be it! if, borne on the bright stream of ages,
    The wreath I have gathered its freshness retain,—
Nor sink, till the chaplets of bards and of sages
    Alike shall be lost in Eternity's main!

BE STILL, MY WILD HEART.

1825.

[On seeing a rural dance at Gargrave feast.]

Be still, my wild heart! in that throb there was sin,
    For each throb of thine is another's by vow;
And the maid 'twas my fortune to woo and to win,
    Was fair as the fairest I look upon now.

As light was her step, and as winningly shy
   Her glances, as any commanding applause ;
And if a slight change hath come over her—why
   Should *he* love her the less who himself is the cause?

All the rapture of hope—all the pain of suspense—
   All the charm of pursuit have been known to my soul ;
And—crowned—shall I view with an envious sense
   The pleasures of those that yet strive for the goal ?

No! 'twas but my heart that, oblivious awhile
   Leaped back to a time when its pulses were free ;
But—awakened—its beatings are true to the smile
Of *Her* whose warm heart is devoted to me !

SHAKE FROM THEE THAT RAIN-DROP.

1825.

[The "spoiler" in the last stanza was my eldest daughter—then a child of a year old.]

SHAKE from thee that rain-drop—as pure as dew,
And open, sweet violet, thy foldings blue!
For the soft shower is over, the sun from the edge
Of the cloud hath streamed out on the young-leaved
   hedge ;

The song of the blackbird is sweet in the larch;
The sky-lark sings clear on the rainbow's high arch;
The breeze is as gentle as breeze may be,
It would sport with, but never would injure thee!

With her varied dress and her soothing hum,
To thee from afar hath the wild bee come;
She hath bent thy stalk—she hath dashed the rain
From thy head—and thy leaves expand again;
And the blended perfumes which spread all around,
Arise from the herbs of the moistened ground,
From sweet-brier bush, and from hawthorn-tree,
Are forgot in the fragrance exhaling from thee!

The bee hath departed to other bowers,
To hum and to banquet on other flowers.
But a surer spoiler now is nigh,
With a rose-bright cheek, and a star-bright eye,
With hair like the sunbeams, and lips—but I pause,
For a father's pencil the portrait draws;
Enough, that no lovelier hand can be,
Than the dear little hand that now seizes thee!

MARK, ELLEN, HOW FAIR.

1826.

Mark, Ellen, how fair on the wild-brier bush
    The last single blossom appears!
A rose of September, that ventures to blush
    Where nothing defends it or cheers.
Though the sun be o'erclouded, the breezes be chill,
    And though bitter showers o'er it have passed,
Round the green boughs that bear it—defying each ill—
    Its balm and its beauty are cast!

And seems it not, Ellen, as lonely it blooms,
    Like the last of our fair summer friends,
Who clings to us still, though the atmosphere glooms,
    And the tempest in fury descends?
Yet it cannot, my love, be an emblem of *thee:*
    When my youth and my fortune are past,
Thy love shall survive, and o'er life's withered tree
    Its balm and its beauty be cast!

I GANG FRAE THEE.

1826.

[I was musing on Northumberland, and humming the air of Macneil's song of "The Way for to Woo," when the last half stanza of the following lyric came spontaneously, as it were, and adapted itself to the music. I thought it good enough to deserve an introduction, which is correct in feeling, though not entirely so in fact.]

I GANG frae thee, gang frae thee sadly,
   Dear land where a bairnie I played;
I gang frae thee, gang frae thee sadly,
   Dear land where my manhood has strayed.
And here in a last look—if tears will but let me—
   I'll bear wi' me far a strang picture o' thee;
And go where I may, I will never forget thee,
   The bonniest lands 'ill kythe barren to me.

   Through vales where my fate bids me wander,
      The streams may flow on wi' mair pride,
   But nae charm will they hae, when I ponder,
      The charms o' my ain Beaumont-Side.
When wave their green woods in the dews o' the morning,
   I'll think o' the lang broom that yellows yon glen;
When they talk o' their high hills and brag o' them scorning,
   I'll think o' the Cheviots, and scorn them again.

My heart has been lang cauld to beauty—
　My first, only love lies in clay!
And I canna allow it a duty,
　My breast that another should sway.
And yet, did I wander the wide warl' ever,
　I should ne'er meet wi' forms nor wi' faces to peer
The clean cottage maids that ted hay by yon river,
　Or lighten the hairst-field wi' laugh and wi' jeer.

Fareweel to thee, land o' my childhood!
　When far frae thy beauties I dee,
My last wish, dear land o' my childhood,
　Shall rise for a blessing on thee—
"Healthy," I'll cry, "gush thy streams frae their
　　fountains,
Birds in thy broomy glens sing the lang day,
Lambs bleat alang the green sides o' thy mountains,
　And lasses bleach claes by ilk bonnie burn-brae!"

BEAUMONT SIDE.

1826.

(On Lanton Hill, as on Howsden, I kept sheep when a boy. It, too, overlooks the Beaumont.)

O BEAUMONT SIDE!—The banks of Aire
　Before that flash of memory fade;
And Lanton Hills are towering there,
　With Newton's vale beneath them laid.

There wave the very rock-sprung trees
  My curious youth with wonder eyed,
And here the long broom scents the breeze—
  The yellow broom of Beaumont Side!

On these hill-tops, at break of day,
  My feet have brushed the pearly dew,
And I have marked the dawn-star's ray
  Lost in the orient's kindling blue;
Then turned to see each neighbouring height
  In Morning's rosy splendours dyed,—
While mists ascending, calm and white,
  Disclosed the banks of Beaumont Side.

No passion then—and unpursued
  The phantom hopes of Love and Fame;
My breast, with piety imbued,
  Admitted—knew—no other flame.
The hill, the stream, the flower, the tree,
  The wandering cloud, and ether wide—
All spoke of glorious things to me,
  The lonely Boy of Beaumont Side!

For then, as yet untaught to scoff
  At all my simple sires believed,
I had not joined the Scorner's laugh,
  Nor night instead of day received.

Amid yon broom, my Bible dear,
    And David's harp my joy and pride,
I felt as Angels hovered near—
    Was half in heaven on Beaumont Side!

But shadows dim the sunniest hill,
    And dark thoughts o'er my spirit sped—
For yonder lay the churchyard still,
    With all its time-collected dead.
And O! to me it seemed so sad
    For ages in the grave to 'bide,
No breeze to blow, no sun to glad!—
    My tears fell fast on Beaumont Side.

"Why weep, fond Boy?" a kind voice said,
    "'Tis but the *shell* that wastes in earth."
I dashed away the tear just shed,
    And knew me of immortal birth!
—I ask not Glory's cup to drain,
    I ask not Wealth's unebbing tide!
O for the INNOCENCE again
    My young heart knew on Beaumont Side!

THE POET'S HOME.

1828.

[On taking possession of a new house in Gargrave.]

'SCAPED from a Hut, much too *poetic*,
Where, plying still his art mimetic,
Sir Spider sits, and looking after
His prey, hangs webs from wall to rafter—
Where he and I, with like enjoyment,
Pursued a similar employment,
That is, both lurked, with few to see us,
He to catch flies, and I ideas,
Which, caught, (to bear the semblance further)
From bard and insect suffered murther.
—'Scaped from that House to one much neater,
Much loftier, roomier, and completer,
(Heaven grant my Landlord cent. per cent.
If he will not enlarge my rent!)
I sit—a reeking glass before me—
A family round that half adore me—
And number up, with mind at ease,
The items of my premises.

And, first, I have a *house*—to hitch in
A rhyme, 'twere better styled a *kitchen*—
Where in my week-day dress I sit,
Laugh at my wife, and show my wit.
The walls yet sparkle to my lamp—
May heaven protect us from the damp!
But if it must destroy one life,
Suppose, just now, it take my wife.
Well, free again. I chat and rove
With Beauty in the moonlight grove,
Till my heart dances to the tune
Sweet of a second Honey Moon.
'Tis a most pleasant thought!——But stay;
Suppose it just the other way—
Suppose it spares my loving wife,
And takes her loving husband's life,
And, further, that another swain
Assumes the matrimonial rein,
And drives the team I drive at present—
By Jove! *this* thought is not so pleasant.

I have a *scullery*, where, each Monday
That comes to sweep the dirt of Sunday,
Finds Ellen, not in best of moods,
Plashing among her frothing suds,
While cock or spigot hourly squirts
The water for the Poet's shirts.

I have a *cellar*—not a deep one,
But yet of depth enough to keep one
A cask or two of gin, or whisky,
Which rhymes to what it makes us—frisky.

My *Parlour* next the verse demands,
A portrait o'er the chimney stands,
But whose? Why mine—by country artist
Ta'en when the Bard was at the smartest,
That is, when in his wedding dress—
And if these tints his face express,
By Phœbus' head! I cannot think
The bard is any common drink.
There's a calm sparkle in the eye,
That speaks somewhat of dignity;
A musing lip; a whisker tight;
A forehead not amiss for height.
It lacks in breath—but this is stuff;
For I have witnessed oft enough
A broader and a loftier sconce
O'ertop the eyebrows of a dunce.
But I digress. For one or two,
My parlour, though but small, will do;
Especially when Ellen's hand
Sets on the board the spirit-stand,
Each bright decanter filled with liquor,
To toast my Landlord and the Vicar;
Or, if a loyal mood it bring,
Old England's patriotic King.

Now, reader, walk up stairs—but hope
Thou not the first-seen door to ope.
The next expand. My girls in this
Dream every night their dreams of bliss,
These snowy curtains round them spread—
Two fairies in a fairy bed!
The third and last, which—half in jest
In earnest half—we style the *best*,
Serves but the hospitable end,
To lodge a stranger or a friend.
Did MITCHELL * leave the Tyne's fair side,
Or GOURLEY † from the Wansbeck ride,
Or HALL,‡ with eloquence at will,
Come from the borders of the Till,—
This chamber should receive, and steep
Their senses in delicious sleep!

I have a *garden*—'tis but small—
Surrounded by a six-foot wall:
Its walks full trim with box and gravel,
On which the nicest foot might travel.
'Tis dark and bare—but come in Spring,
These elms shall then no shadow fling!
These walls with blossom clothed shall be
By many an autumn-planted tree;
While many a garden flower smiles by,
To lure the bee and butterfly!

---

* Mitchell—the editor of the Newcastle Magazine. † Gourley—master of the Corporation School, Morpeth. ‡ Hall—the dissenting-minister of Crookham.—All good-hearted men, and all now under the turf.

Such my new Residence; and yet
It was with something like regret
I left the old one!—There, I've been
For years contented and serene;
There bloomed my girls—the damps it shed
Ne'er turned to pale their cherub red;
And there my rapt and musing eye,
Touched by the *glamour*, Poesy!
Hath ta'en its rude and ochre'd wall
For one belonging princely hall,
And every cobweb's waving fold
For cloth of silver or of gold!
Yes! it is certain, that the bard
To house or hall pays light regard.
Where'er he dwelleth—be his roof
Pervious to storm or tempest-proof—
There throng the shapes his magic raised,
There bend the forms his songs have praised,
Unseen by all but him, they come,
Brighten his light, or gild his gloom—
And, blest with these, the same his lot,
Whether in Castle or in Cot!

THERE'S A DARK HOUR COMING.

1828.

[Reflecting on the fate of poor John S——, of Humbleton. His love was a Miss H——, of Wooler, and to her I conceived he might have thus addressed himself.]

There's a dark hour coming,
   Which thou, so kind and dear,
In all thy beauty blooming,
   Shalt fail to charm or cheer!
The shade it casts before it,
   Its very shade is drear—
And my soul as it comes o'er it,
   Feels a deep, prophetic fear!
     There's a dark hour coming!

The honour oft applauded,
   The heart all truth to thee,
The genius men have lauded
   Will soon be lost in me.
A star at once o'erclouded,
   Whose beam was fair to see—
The sun in darkness shrouded—
   O! *nought* can emblem be
     Of the dark hour coming!

Its charm when friendship loses,
    When love is felt no more;
When glory and the Muses
    Have seen their influence o'er;
When I view with hate or terror
    The friends I loved before,
When my laugh they hear with horror
    And, unthanked, my state deplore,—
    O! that dark hour's coming!

ONE APRIL MORN.

1828.

[Roddam Dean was the "valley"—not properly so called—that "bloomed before me."]

One April morn I musing lay,
    My eyelids closed without my knowing—
Above me was a sky-lark gay,
    Beside me was a streamlet flowing.

That bird seemed just the very bird
    In mine own land that caroled o'er me!
That streamlet's voice the same I heard
    When one sweet valley bloomed before me.

I started—to my feet I sprung
  As if to find my former world;
—'Twas but a Craven bird that sung,
  'Twas but a Craven stream that purled!

REPLY TO AN EPISTLE FROM MR. GOURLEY.

1828.

(Mr. Gourley, already mentioned in a note, was a self-taught mathematician, and a thirty years' intimate friend and correspondent of mine.)

DEAR SIR,
    Your favour reached me duly,
For which, of course, I thank you truly,
And now address me to the task
Of answering all you kindly ask.

"How are you?" Well. "And how your wife?"
Never was better in her life.
"Thank God! But for another query,
Your children, how?" Alive and merry.

"Prolonged be every pure enjoyment!
And now, what is the Bard's employment?
Spends he his time, as usual, gaily?
Or, settled to a plodder daily,
Centres his every scheme in self,
His only object grasping pelf?
Is Poesy his loved pursuit?
And if so, when will come the *Fruit?*
The *Blossoms** lived a single day
Then passed—like other flowers—away.

Say will the *Fruit*, when gathered, cheer
Our banquets for at least a year?
How stand your politics? I know it,
The politics of genuine poet
May with propriety be ta'en
Rather as light whims of the brain,
Than principles by labour wrought
From the deep mine of solid Thought.
But do you stand a red-hot tory?
Or, floating with the tide, will Story
Seek (to adopt the day's expression)
The calmer harbour of *concession?*
Your thoughts, opinions, freely state'em."
Then, here they follow *seriatim.*

First, of employment I've enough,
Of avocations *quantum suff.*

* A small collection of poems entitled "Craven Blossoms."

Like Goldsmith's juggler, when one trick
Begins to make the public sick,
I'm able from my treasured store,
To try them with a hundred more.
And sooth to tell without dissembling
I sometimes see with fear and trembling
The likelihood, in spite of all
My hundred tricks, of sudden fall;
And envy, in my dread of failure,
The destiny of common Tailor!

You long have known me "skilled to rule,"
As master of a village school.
A useful post, but thankless still—
Of which the ancients thought so ill,
They held the man to whom 'twas given,
An object of the wrath of heaven.
—By fools beset, by idiots judged,
His pains despised, his payments grudged,
Rivalled by *things*, whom juster doom
Had placed in farm-yard or at loom,
(For 'tis as true as parsons preach
That men who ne'er were taught, can teach!)
Hard is his lot, to own the truth,
Condemned to train our rising youth.
Yet even in this picture dark
The eye some streaks of light may mark—
The common mob, whose grovelling nature
Would for Hyperion choose a Satyr,

By loftier mind or station awed,
Will *sometimes* properly applaud,
Following, like sheep, the judging few—
And lucky Merit gets his due.

Learn, next, that I am Parish Clerk—
A noble office, by St. Mark!
It brings me in six guineas clear,
Besides *et ceteras*, every year.
I waive my Sunday duty, when
I give the solemn, deep Amen,
Exalted there to breathe aloud
The heart-devotion of the crowd.
But O the fun! when Christmas-chimes
Have ushered in the festal times,
And sent the Clerk and Sexton round
To pledge their friends in draughts profound,
And keep on foot the good old plan,
As only Clerk and Sexton can!
Nor less the sport, when Easter sees;
The daisy spring to deck the leas;
Then, claimed as dues by Mother Church,
I pluck the cackler from the perch;
Or, in its place, the shilling clasp
From grumbling Dame's slow-opening grasp.

But, Visitation-day! 'tis thine
Best to deserve my votive line—
Great Day! the purest, brightest gem
That decks the Year's fair diadem!

Grand Day! that sees me costless dine,
And costless quaff the rosy wine,
Till seven Church-wardens doubled seem,
And doubled every candle's gleam,
And I—triumphant over time,
And over tune, and over rhyme—
Called by the gay, convivial throng,
Lead, in full glee, the choral song!
—I love thee, brandy, on my soul;
And, rum, thou'rt precious in the bowl;
Whisky is dear, because it tells
Of the bright dew of Scottish fells;
But nought commands the poet's praise
Like wine—for which the Parish pays!

For Song—'tis still my loved pursuit,
And you shall soon possess the *Fruit*.
But whether it will *keep*, to cheer
Your banquets for a month, or year,
Let time decide—or sages pure
That sentence give on literature.
—Critics in every age have tried
The endless question to decide
Of "What is Poetry?" and still
It busies many a learned quill.
Poets themselves, seduced to quit
Their high and native walks of wit,
Have stooped to cramp and to confine,

In school-taught terms, their Art Divine,—
When they had best performed their part,
And honoured most their glorious art,
By pointing out some passage, fraught
With Taste, with Genius, and with Thought,
Where heart, and soul, and fancy give
Their mingling hues to glow and live—
And saying: "Find who will the *why*,
But this, we feel, is Poetry."
Thus I, who little heed the rules
By critics made for rhyming fools,
Have formed, though o'er my second bottle,
As sure a test as Aristotle—
Read Shakspeare's glowing page to see
What *is* undoubted poetry;
And then *this paragraph*, God wot,
If you would see—what it is *not*.

My Harp was made from stunted tree,
The growth of Glendale's barest lea;
Yet fresh as prouder stems it grew,
And drank, with leaf as green, the dew;
Bright showers, from Till or Beaumont shed,
Its roots with needful moisture fed;
Gay birds, Northumbrian skies that wing,
Amid its branches loved to sing;
And purple Cheviot's breezy air
Kept up a life-like quivering there.

From Harp thence framed, and rudely strung,
Can aught but lowly strain be flung?
No! if, ambition led, I dream
Of striking it to lofty theme,
All harshly jar its tortured chords
As plaining such should be its lord's;
But all its sweetness waketh still
To lay of Border stream or hill!

To CRAVEN's emerald dales transferred,
That simple Harp with praise is heard.
The manliest sons, the loveliest daughters
That flourish by the Aire's young waters,
By hurrying Ribble's verdant side,
And by the Wharf's impetuous tide,
Laud its wild strains. And, for this cause,
While throbs my breast to kind applause—
Nay, when, beneath the turf laid low,
No kind applause my breast can know,
The *Poet's blessing*, heart-bequeathed,
O'er thy domains, green CRAVEN! breathed,
Shall be to every hill and plain
Like vernal dew, or summer rain,
And stay with thee, while bud or bell
Decks lowland mead or upland fell!

Thus have I scribbled on, my friend,
Till Ellen hints 'tis time to end;
My nails worn to the quick with gnawing,
My caput sore with—with—with *clawing*.

(What words we bards are forced, at times,
To press into the corps of rhymes!)
My conscience, how the quizzer laughs!
During the last two paragraphs,
These symptoms, as poetic known,
She says have quite outrageous grown;
And threatens or to quench my taper,
O'erturn my ink, or burn my paper.
So to prevent these doings rude,
I think it better to conclude,
And aught unanswered or perplexed,
To clear and answer in my next.
Meantime I wish you Peace—Love—Glory!
And am,
    Yours ever,
      ROBERT STORY.

TWENTY YEARS PARTED.

1828.

[My father, in his grave, is supposed to address my mother—just laid beside him.]

Twenty years parted,
   Though forty years tried,
And found still true-hearted—
   Return to my side!
And quiet and deep
Shall be thy long sleep
Where the heart is at rest, and the tear is dried!

From trials and woes
   That so long have been thine,
Come, taste the repose
   Which the grave hath made mine—
And quiet and deep
Shall be thy long sleep
Where no blast ever comes, if no sunbeam shine!

With want, one long strife
   'Twas our lot to maintain,
Till we quitted a life
   Undisgraced by a stain;

But quiet and deep
Shall be our long sleep,
Till the last Morn's dawn see us wake again!

BREATHE, BREATHE ON MY HEART.

1829.

[On revisiting Roddam Dean.]

BREATHE, breathe on my heart, O breathe on my heart,
  Ye flowers of a valley so loved of yore!
I come but to gaze—but to gaze and depart,
  And I ask ye the pulse of my youth to restore!
For my heart is so languid, so weary, so low,
So dry, and so withered!—But breathe as ye blow,
Your beauty into it—cool—dewy—and Oh!
  It will waken to all its old feelings once more.

"Breathe, breathe on my heart, sweet crow-flower, breathe,
  As thou streakest the turf with the gold of thy bloom!
And ye, purple blossoms, that gem the dark heath,
  O freshen my soul with your mountain perfume!

The primrose hath vanished; the violet too,
Hath passed from the walk with its leaflets of blue;
And of all the gay blossoms of broomwood, but few
   Remain with their light in the glen's verdant gloom.

"Yet breathe on my heart, ye lingerers, breathe!
   Ye have rapture within your moist foldings for me!
And thou, stately fox-glove, thyself a bright wreath
   Of blossoms the loveliest, I call upon thee;
From thy string of sweet bells—a most fairy-like
   string—
The soft, silent music of beauty O fling!
It will enter my heart like a song in the spring—
   The first that is poured from the fresh-budding tree!

"Breathe, breathe on my heart, wild thyme of the
   hill,
   That lovest to bloom on the verge of the glen!
Breathe, every sweet floweret befringing the rill,
   Or namelessly starring the green of the fen!
But chiefly, ye roses, profusely that flaunt,
Ye woodbines, that welcome me back to my haunt,
The charm and the perfume of other years grant—
   O breathe on my heart as ye breathed on it then!"

I stood, as I spoke, on the brow of the dell,
   Where oft I had loitered in long vanished years;
And here waved the forest, and there rose the fell,
   Which the songs of my youth had described without
   peers!

The flowers I apostrophised, over me cast
The sweets they had shed in the bright summers past,
And, o'ercome by the reflux of feeling at last,
    I sank on the turf, and bedewed it with tears!

THE DEAD STOOD BY.

1830.

[The "two youthful friends" in the following stanzas, were William Thompson, a fellow-reaper in the fields of Roddam, and John Smith, of Humbleton. The "lovely vision" was Jeanie Kennedy, of Reveley, on the Breamish.]

The Dead stood by my couch last night!
    (The living of another sphere!)
And my raised spirit, at the sight,
    Felt much of awe, but nought of fear;
For though, e'en in my dream, I knew
    Immortal Forms bent o'er my bed,
They were so like themselves! the true—
    The fair—the reverenced!—Could I dread?

So like themselves! and yet they had
    A look they wore not when alive—
It was not stern, it was not sad,
    Though sternness seemed with grief to strive.

I

It was a mournful seriousness—
   A pity grave—most like the air
Which, when compassion they express,
   We deem an Angel's eyes may wear!

A tall old man stood next my face—
   Well in his thin, dark, furrowed cheek,
And forehead mild, my soul could trace
   The features loved in childhood weak.
I thought on the paternal cot—
   The circle round its evening flame—
And my lips moved, but murmured not—
   I could not speak my Father's name!

Two youthful Friends beside him stood,
   Whom early death had snatched away;
The *one*—of those who humbly good,
   Seek the mild virtues to display.
He moved in no eccentric course,
   Allured by Passion or by Pride;
He knew no vice, felt no remorse,
   But meekly lived, and calmly died.

The *other*—O how different He!
   Him Genius cherished as a son;
Th' unfading wreath of Poesy
   He looked on as already won.

Through untried regions plumed to range,
    His muse had just essayed to fly,
When he exchanged—a great exchange!—
    Glory on earth, for bliss on high.

A once-loved Form stood next and last,
    A lovely vision—pure—and still—
Whose living charms had all surpassed
    That bloomed by Breamish or by Till.
She seemed no fairer than of old,—
    But then there was a *fixedness*
Of beauty on her cheek, that told
    It never could be more—or less!

My very heart within me yearned
    To see these visitants divine;
Nor was it long before I learned
    Their spirits held discourse with mine!
There was no word, or turn of eye;
    Upon my ear no music stole;
But yet there was communion high—
    The silent talk of soul with soul!

My past career they marked with blame,
    Its thoughtless faults, its deeper crimes;
They bade me quit the race of Fame,
    And run for nobler prize than Time's.

"The fame," they said, "by man bestowed,
    Fills not the high immortal soul;
The glorious wreath conferred by God,
    Shall bloom—when earth has ceased to roll!

"Death is at hand—that throwing down
    Of barriers which the soul confine—
When the pure heart shall gain a crown:
    Why not that heavenly crown be *thine?*
By prayer—by prayer—unfile thy heart,
    And join us in eternity!—
For O! retain this truth—Thou art,
    And never canst thou cease to be!"*

* These words form the moral of "The Pelican Island"—the finest of all the fine poems of James Montgomery.

"Thou art, and thou canst never cease to be!

O WOMAN, FAIR WOMAN.

1830.

O Woman, fair Woman, thou breakest on man
  As the dawn of a bright summer day
Shines forth on a vapour uncoloured and wan,
  And kindles it up by its ray—
Till quite metamorphosed, it rests in the sky,
  A radiant and purified thing—
And meet, as it seemeth to Fancy's bold eye,
  An Angel to lure on the wing!

O Woman, fair Woman, thou breakest on man,
  Like that summer dawn beaming above,
And man is that vapour uncoloured and wan,
  Till touched and illumed by thy love.
Then, changed and enkindled, he glows in thine eye,
  From all that degraded him free—
High-thoughted, and pure as the cloud in the sky,
  Yet wishing no Angel but Thee!

IT IS SWEET TO PERCEIVE.

1831.

It is sweet to perceive the first efforts of Spring;
    To watch the buds tenderly, timidly ope;
To feel at one's heart the pure freshness they bring,
    Till the languid heart leaps to the promise of Hope!
Of spring talks yon blue sky, of spring this green land,
    Of spring the gay warblings these valleys that fill—
Sweet proof that the Mighty Artificer's hand
    Impels the machine of the universe still!

God! dost thou not rule in the armies of heaven?
    Thy impulse the stars in their courses obey;
The lightnings themselves, when the dark cloud is riven
    Flash fate as thou biddest, or harmlessly play!
And hast thou relinquished the curb and control
    Of man? Hath thy government ceased from the world?
Then whence this unquietness, madness of soul?
    And why are those ensigns of battle unfurled?

O! with the strong voice that can still the wild sea,
    Speak peace to the hearts and the passions of men!
With the power that hath bidden the winter-clouds flee
    Let the sunshine of joy gild their dwellings again!

And with the soft breath that awakens the spring,
    Breathe over the mind of the nations, O Lord!
That genuine freedom which comes not from king,
    Nor is won, or destroyed, by the conqueror's sword!

But if, for some purpose inscrutable, Thou
    Wilt see over Europe wild Anarchy burst,
O! let not my country her honoured neck bow
    To the yoke of that Despot—the vilest—the worst!
Give wisdom to guard our old strengths that have stood
    The beatings of time, as her rocks the rude sea,
And Albion shall ever o'erlook the blue flood,
    The first of the nations—the Isle of the Free!

O! BLEST IS THE HEARTH.

1832.

O Blest is the hearth, and delightful the home
    Where Honour and Virtue preside;
Where the Husband's as kind as the youthful Bridegroom,
    And the Wife is as fond as the Bride!

Though the bloom may be fading that lived on *her*
    cheek,
And the fire of *his* glance may be colder,
The MIND still is there, true affection to speak,
    And the mind never grows any older!

THE FEW CORN FIELDS.

1832.

[These lines were addressed to Margaret, or, as I liked better to call her, PEGGY Richardson, a young and pretty girl of Calder, on the Roddam estate, with whom I reaped more than one harvest, and who was the heroine of a juvenile poem of mine.]

THE few corn-fields that Craven sees
    Like patches on her landscape green,
Wave yellow now in sun and breeze,
    Inviting out the sickle keen.

But who the sickle bears afield?
    I see no fair and youthful band,
The peaceful weapon prompt to wield,
    And clear—with mirth—the waving land.

A single reaper—(past belief!)
    Plies awkwardly his lonely toil;
He makes the band, he binds the sheaf,
    And rears the shock—without a smile!

Yet e'en this sight of single field
    And single reaper, brings to me
A mood to which I like to yield—
    A dream of Roddam fields and thee.

On Roddam's harvest land, who now
    Bid the hot day unheeded fly?
Is there a Maiden fair as thou?
    Is there a Lover fond as I?

Dost recollect—when, side by side,
    'Twas ours to lead the jovial band—
With what delight, and heart-felt pride,
    I saw thee grace my dexter hand!

Dost recollect—'mid sickles' jar—
    How rang, at jests, the laughter-chorus?
Our line, the while, extending far,
    And driving half a field before us!

Dost recollect, at resting-time,
    Announced by Roddam's village clock,
(Methinks e'en now I hear the chime!)
    The *squeeze* beside the yellow shock?

Dost recollect, when evening came,
   The dance got up with ready glee?
How active grew each wearied frame!
   How lightly *then* I danced with thee.

Dost recollect—when half asleep
   Thy mother and thy grumbling sire—
The pleasant watch we used to keep
   For hours beside the smothered fire?

For e'en the fair Moon's radiance pure,
   That trembled through the window blue,
Along the cottage furniture
   Too strong a light—for lovers—threw.

But where art thou? and where am I?
   And Roddam's corn-fields, where are they?
Ah! where the days when thou wert nigh,
   The rainbow of my darkest day?

For fair thou wert; though ne'er, perchance,
   So fair as my young fancy drew thee;—
I see, e'en yet, the roguish glance
   That linked my captive heart unto thee!

And when I think of thee, I scarce
   Can think of thee as differing aught
From her who once inspired my verse—
   Though in *myself* a change is wrought.

The reaper's part that once I bore
    Untired, I could not bear again;
And did thy sire make fast the *door*,
    I could not enter at the *pane*.

The toilsome day would slowly pass;
    Reflection nought could bring but woe;
And for the evening dance, alas!
    One Scottish reel would make me blow.

Suppose us met in Roddam field—
    I verging to my fortieth year,
And thou not far behind—to wield,
    As once we did, the sickle clear.

We could not choose but laugh—or weep;
    The last would be my first employment,
To feel emotions—long asleep—
    Re-wakening but to *past* enjoyment?

Is that the hand I loved to grasp?
    Thine cannot be that cheek so wan!
Nor thine that waist! I used to clasp
    A waist that my two hands could span!

Alas! the truth we *might* have known,
    But *would* not, flashes on us now—
That YOUTH MUST FLY; for it *hath* flown,
    And ceased to love have I and thou!

On Roddam fields another race
    The part we took of old, have ta'en;
They toil—or toy—in each dear place
    That ne'er shall meet our glance again?

Thus when a boy on Beaumont Side,
    (A scene that is not strange to thee)
I saw the heath-bloom in its pride
    Bend to the kiss of mountain bee:

And bees and blooms, no doubt, are rife
    By Beaumont still; but never—never—
Shall *those* I saw in early life
    Be seen again by that sweet river!

—Well; time does but to us award
    The fate by millions felt before;
And *I am Roddam's youthful bard,*
    Thou Calder's fairest flower no more!

AGAIN THE SWEETEST SEASON.

1832.

Again the sweetest season wakes,
    Again the bud is on the tree—
A sight, my Ellen, which it makes
    Me pleased and sad at once, to see.

"I feel the joy which Nature feels,
    As in my youth's departed prime;
I feel—what every shrub reveals—
    The tender beauty of the time.

"But ah! to think—while Nature keeps
    All unimpaired her mighty power,
Clothing as richly plains and steeps
    As in the earth's primeval hour—

"To think that I, if natural length
    Of years withhold me from the urn,
With feebler pulse and waning strength,
    Must hail each future spring's return!

"To think that, laid at last in clay,
    No more for me shall earth be clad
In all the young spring's fresh array—
    My spirit sinks, and I am sad!

Prompt was my Ellen's kind reply
    To check the low, despondent strain:
" Nay, for a smile exchange that sigh,"
    She said, " and triumph, not complain!

" Spring-flowers are types of human bliss,
    So beautiful—so frail their forms:
Nor do we name our woes amiss—
    The blight of frosts, the crush of storms.

" Our spring-time flies with smile and song,
    Swift as the sun-gleam o'er the lea;
But O! What words may tell the long,
    Dark, winter-time, of *misery* ?

" From life's long blast 'twere very sweet
    To feel, with every spring that blows,
We draw more near the calm retreat
    In which the weary find repose.

" But shall we stoop from Paynim founts
    To draw the solace Paynims drew?
No, no! the Christian's spirit mounts,
    And soars above yon vault of blue.

" There sees, in a serener clime,
    A fairer spring evolve its bloom,
Untarnished by one touch of time—
    Unsaddened by a single tomb!

"Where happy souls—their troubles o'er,
    Their weariness and worldly strife—
Bathe in the streams for evermore
    Whose every *swell* is bliss and life!

"Now, love, exult, to think, with me,
    Each spring but sees us nearer rise
To that Land of Felicity
    Its beauty faintly typifies!"

WETHERCOTE CAVE.

1833.

[This is a remarkable fissure in a rock, rather than a cave, into which a torrent is constantly poured. I was forcibly struck with the contrast between this scene of noise and tumult, and the quiet and silence of the church and churchyard of Chapel-le-Dale, which are within a little distance of it.]

This rugged descent, and this horror sublime,
The gloom of these caves excavated by Time;
This far fall of waters which, crushed by their fall,
Are hovering—in mist—round each moss-covered
    wall;
The roar of their tortures, ere upward they swell
Over rocks that seem tinted with colours of Hell!—
And these shadows shall lour, and these waters shall
    rave,
Till the last trumpet echoes o'er Wethercote cave!

What calmer, what holier emotions prevail
In the breast that beholds *thee*, sweet Chapel-le-Dale!
And O! when I think on the struggle, the strife,
The pomp, and the pride, and the nonsense of life,
And know that all ends, when the turmoil is past,
In the quiet and calm of the churchyard at last,—
The toils of the learned, and the feats of the brave,
Seem the vain noise of waters in Wethercote cave!

WITH BOUNDING STEP.

1833.

[These lines are founded on the following fact:—Some thirty years ago, two boys, sons of a gentleman in Malham, left their home in search of birds' nests. Arriving at the top of a lofty crag, called CAM SCAR, the elder, an adventurous little fellow of five or six years old, descended the tremendous precipice, and having secured a hawk's nest, was returning to the summit, when, stooping to pluck a knot of cowslips, he lost his hold and fell. His brother, too young to understand what had happened, found his body at the foot of the rock, and after repeatedly shaking it, returned home, quite unconcerned. "I shook him very hard," said he, in answer to his father's inquiries, "but he was SOUND ASLEEP."]

With bounding step, and laughing eye,
   Young Edgar sprang his sire to hail—
The child had rambled far and high
   Among the crags of Malhamdale.—

"See, father, what a pretty wreath
  Of flowers!—I would their names I knew!—
I found this bright one on the heath,
  Its golden leaves all moist with dew.

"This, father, is a primrose pale,
  I knew it in its hazel bower—
But every child within the dale
  Knows, as I think, the primrose-flower.

"O, this small bud 'twas hard to spy!
  Deep in a mossy cleft it grew:
With nought to look at, save the sky,
  It seems to have imbibed its blue!"

Not yet, perchance, had Edgar stayed
  The prattle, to a parent dear;
But—"Why," the anxious father said,
  "Is Henry, with *his* flowers, not here?"

"My brother? O, I had forgot,"
  The little rosy boy replied,
"I left him in the wildest spot—
  Asleep—yon mighty crag beside."

"Asleep, my boy?"—"Yes, father. We
  A hawk had startled from a chink;
And, on the crag's top leaving me,
  My brother clambered round its brink.

"Soon did I hear his shout of glee—
　The nest became his instant prize;
When clambering back his way to me,
　A knot of cowslips caught his eyes.

"He stooped, and disappeared. Some time
　I stood and watched the hazel shoot,
By which my brother up might climb;
　At last I sought the crag's green foot.

"I found him lying on the sward,
　The grassy sward beneath the steep;
I shook, and shook him very hard—
　But, father, he was sound asleep."

The father shrieked the lost one's name!
　Young Edgar heard, and held his breath;
For o'er him, with a shudder, came
　The thought that he had been with—Death

He led them to the fatal spot,
　Where, still and cold, his brother lay,
Within his hand the cowslip knot
　That lured his heedless foot astray.

That cowslip-knot shall never pour
　Its sweets again on summer gale,
And that poor boy shall never more
　Climb the wild crags of Malhamdale.

I KNOW THOU LOV'ST ME.

1834.

[Written after reading some sermons by the late Dr. Adam Clarke.]

I know thou lov'st me, hast at heart
   My mortal and immortal weal;
That mine hath been a thankless part,
   I bitterly and deeply feel.

Pure was the light that filled my soul
   In boyhood—for the light was thine;
But soon, too soon did error roll
   Its darkness o'er the brilliant shine.

In pride of heart, as manhood came,
   I sought me paths abhorred by thee;
Forsook thy worship and thy name;—
   But thou hast ne'er forsaken me;

My Father's God! I recollect
   Escapes in that abandoned time,
And own and bless the hand that checked
   My course upon the *verge of crime*.

Was this not for my Father's sake?
   For thus of old thy promise ran,
That thou wouldst ne'er thy favour take
   From offspring of the righteous man.

In bloom of being, one by one,
   I saw my young companions die;
Thy work in me was not begun—
   I was unfitted for the sky!

Yet not by shock of crushing ill
   Spok'st thou "in thunder" from above;
To me thy Mercy—in the "still,
   Small voice" of *blessings*—whispered love.

The hand that made the heart, full well
   Its nature knows. Like early rain,
On mine's dry soil thy goodness fell,
   And made it soft to bloom again!

Blest in my basket and my store,
   Blest in my children, wife and home,
I *feel* thou lov'st me—and no more
   Would I from thee perversely roam.

THE ISLES ARE AWAKE!

1834.

[These lines were first published in the STANDARD of December 10, 1834, and were thence transferred to the pages of every Conservative newspaper in the three kingdoms. During the General Election of 1835, they were again brought out, and again they made the tour of the periodical press. In South Lancashire, in particular, many thousand copies of them were circulated; and having been hitherto printed anonymously, they were now attributed to the Earl of Ellesmere—(then Lord Francis Egerton)—one of the successful candidates for the representation of that district. His lordship's disclaimer of the authorship was made in a way highly gratifying to the real writer, and led to the dedication of a collection of my poems to his lordship.]

HARK! heard ye that sound as it passed in the gale?
And saw ye not yonder Destructive turn pale?
'Twas the heart-shout of Loyalty, fervent and true;
'Twas the death-knell of Hope to himself and his crew:
O waft it, ye breezes, and far let it ring,
That the Isles are awake at the voice of the King!

Long years have passed over, in which, with a sigh,
The good man looked on as the wicked sat high;
And half he forgot, in the depth of his grief,
That the joy of the bad hath the date of a leaf:
Thank God, it is blighted! and true men may sing,
Since the Isles are awake at the voice of the King!

The tide of our love never ebbs. We loved on,
When the gloom of ill counsels o'ershadowed his
    throne ;
We loved, when the sun of our Monarch grew dim ;
We sorrowed, yet not for ourselves, but for him ;
And self hath small part in the raptures that spring
To see the Isles wake at the voice of the King !

He hath spoke like his Father—"THE ALTAR SHALL
    STAND !"
Which England re-echoes from mountain to strand ;
The dark heaths of Scotia the burden prolong,
And the green dales of Erin burst out into song ;
For her harpies of strife and of blood have ta'en wing,
And the Isles are awake at the voice of the King !

THE CHURCH OF OUR FATHERS.

1835.

[This lyric followed immediately on the preceding one, and was almost equally popular. Set to music by Robert Guylott.]

ENCIRCLED by trees, in the Sabbath's calm smile,
    The church of our fathers—how meekly it stands !
O villagers, gaze on the old, hallowed pile—
    It was dear to their hearts, it was raised by their
        hands !

Who loves not the place where they worshipped
    their God?
Who loves not the ground where their ashes repose!
Dear even the daisy that blooms on the sod,
    For dear is the dust out of which it arose!

Then say, shall the church that our forefathers built,
    Which the tempests of ages have battered in vain,
Abandoned by us from supineness or guilt,
    O say, shall it fall by the rash and profane?
No!—Perish the impious hand that would take
    One shred from its altar, one stone from its towers!
The life-blood of Martyrs hath flowed for its sake,
    And its fall, if it fall—shall be reddened with ours.

THE BRIDE IS AWAY.

1835.

[On the marriage of Miss M——, of the vicarage, Gargrave. Set to music by Richard Limpus, Jun.]

The Bride is away—and there does not breathe one
    Within the glad sound of these bells,
Who feels not as if with that lady were gone
    Some charm from the spot where he dwells;

There does not breathe one but who feels at his heart
    Two currents of sentiment met,
And who hardly knows whether the tear that would start
    Is the offspring of Joy or Regret!

The Bride is away—like a bird from the bower,
    In which 'twas the sweetest that sung;
Like a flower she hath passed, like a violet flower,
    That perfumed all the place where it sprung!
And she charms other hearts with her bloom and her song,
    But though of her presence bereft,
The thought of her goodness and loveliness long
    Will be sweet in the hearts she hath left!

STOP, O STOP THE PASSING-BELL.

1835.

(I heard the passing-bell one morning. It was tolling for Mrs. Coulthurst, of Gargrave House—a lady respected by all. "What must her husband feel to hear these sounds?" I said, and wrote the lines.)

Stop, O stop the passing-bell!
    Painfully, too painfully,
It strikes against the heart, that knell;
I cannot bear its tones—they tell
    Of misery, of misery!
All that soothed and sweetened life
In the Mother and the Wife—
All that would a charm have cast
O'er the future as the past—
All is torturing in that knell!
Stop, O stop the passing-bell.

Stop it—no! But change the tone,
    And joyfully, ay, joyfully,
Let the altered chimes ring on,
For the spirit that hath flown
    Exultingly, exultingly!
She hath left her couch of pain;
She shall never feel again

But as angels feel—afar
Climed beyond the morning star,
Agony and death unknown!
Let the joyful chimes ring on!

THE WIVES AND THE MOTHERS OF BRITAIN.

1835.

[Set to music by — Johnson, of Preston, in Lancashire, and—for private circulation—by Elias Chadwick, Esq., then of Swinton Hall, Manchester.]

Let each fill his glass, fill it up to the brim,
   For my toast is well worthy a full one,
Nor would I give much for the feelings of him
   Who should deem it a vapid and dull one:
For him not a wine cup deservedly foams,
   Whatever gay room he may sit in;
I give you the WOMEN that brighten our homes—
   "The Wives and the Mothers of Britain!"

'Tis a toast comprehensive—it leaves no one out
   Whose smiles make an English hearth pleasant,
From the fair cottage-matron that, rosy and stout,
   Delights the bold heart of the peasant—

From her to the dame of the stateliest hall
    Our proudest nobility sit in,
And up to the Queen, who presides over all,
    The Wives and the Mothers of Britain!

Nor will we forget the sweet rose-buds that blow
    Beneath the kind eye of those mothers;
Whose hearts are their own, yet not long may be so,
    But devotedly, meekly, another's.
Let us hope that their sons will be patriots true,
    Like those of the room that we sit in;
And still be it felt there is reverence due
    To the Wives and the Mothers of Britain!

THE WANE OF THE DAY.

1835.

(This was a birth-day Song, written on completing my fortieth year. I fancied myself old.)

O the heart is not so light
    In the wane of the day,
And the eye is not so bright
    In the wane of the day;

The ear hath duller grown
　　For the swell of music's tone,
And the dance's charm is gone
　　In the wane of the day!

The sweet spring hath its buds
　　In the wane of the day,
Where the primrose decks the woods
　　In the wane of the day;
The mead is flushed with gold,
And the lark is on the wold,
But he sings not as of old—
　　In the wane of the day!

Yet I have some ties to life
　　In the wane of the day;
I've a fair and frugal wife
　　In the wane of the day;
And when round my evening hearth
Mix my little band in mirth,
I'm the happiest man on earth
　　In the wane of the day!

THE ANCIENT BARONS.

1836.

("Nolumus leges Angliæ mutari!" was the patriotic declaration of the Ancient Barons to King John. This lyric has been set to music by J. P. Knight.)

The ancient Barons of the land
    Composed a haughty ring,
When—mail on breast and blade in hand—
    They stood before the King;
And, dauntless in their country's cause,
    Their high resolve avowed—
"WE WILL NOT THAT OLD ENGLAND'S LAWS
    BE CHANGED BY COURT OR CROWD!

"In other lands, at slightest shock,
    The civil fabric falls;
In ours eternal as the rock,
    It rears its massive walls;
A barrier to convulsion forms,
    Firm as our Island's shore,
Which has rolled back ten thousand storms,
    And will ten thousand more!

"To guard its towers from age to age,
    Brave men their last have breathed;
To us, as our best heritage,
    It was by them bequeathed.

And, mark us, Sire! to its defence
　　Our arms—our lives—we vow :
And it may fall in ages hence—
　　We Swear it shall not now!"

They kept their oath, those gallant men!
　　The structure still is ours,
Though twice three hundred years since then
　　Have overswept its towers.
A glorious barrier still it forms,
　　Firm as our Island's shore,
Which has rolled back ten thousand storms,
　　And *shall* ten thousand more!

IT IS SAD, VERY SAD.

1836.

(I had been at Liverpool. It was night, and there was deep snow on the ground. While coming over Blackstone edge, in a stage coach, I wrote these lines.)

It is sad, very sad, thus without thee to roam;
It is sad, very sad, when the heart is at home!
My dearest—yes, DEAREST! that word it shall be,
For it has a sweet meaning when spoken of thee!
　　　　My dearest, yes, DEAREST! &c.

My dearest, I've been where the wild billows roll,
And I am where the scene should enrapture my soul
But, unmoved by the beauties of land and of sea,
My soul finds them tasteless—ungazed on by thee! ;
    My dearest, yes, DEAREST! &c.

Are my girls and my boys all as rosy and gay,
Is my kind wife as well as when I came away?
Are ever the questions returning to me;
And soon be they answered by them and by thee!
  My dearest, yes, DEAREST! that word it shall be,
  For it has a sweet meaning when spoken of thee!

THE FRIENDS THAT I LOVED.

1836.

The friends that I loved I love still—but no more
Those friends of my bosom illumine my door;
O! what can it be that has made them so cold,
Who bore me such love and affection of old?

My soul is the same—by misfortune unbowed,
It pities the poor, it despises the proud;
And still are my feelings the same as of old;
O! what can it be that has made them so cold?

It is true that my visage is pallid and worn—
It is true that my garments are faded and torn—
And perhaps I'm so altered, they cannot descry
The man at whose table they feasted so high!

I was once of each party the life and the soul,
My sallies were voted as bright as my bowl;
And sometimes the reason I bitterly ask,
Why the wit left my head when the wine left my cask?

Well, mind them not, Ellen!—One friend I have still,
Who, kind in good fortune, is kinder in ill;
And whose smile, like a glimpse of the sun in a shower,
Can brighten Adversity's gloomiest hour!

SWEET BEAUMONT SIDE.

1836.

[Set to a very beautiful air by my late friend Mr. Wood, of Gargrave, and published with accompaniments by J. W. Thirlwall.]

Sweet Beaumont Side, and Beaumont Stream!
    Though winds of winter round me blow,
I cannot think, I cannot dream,
    With *you* that it is ever so.
On Flasby Fell the blast may rave,
    The drift may whirl on Frozen Aire;
No winter binds the Beaumont's wave,
    No storm enshrouds a mountain there!

Sweet Beaumont Side, and Beaumont Stream!
    Ye come to me in visions clear,
And ever as ye were ye seem;
    Change cannot touch a scene so dear!
On Howsden heights for ever bloom,
    The flowers that lure the mountain bee;
By Beaumont Side the yellow broom
    For ever waves—in light—to me!

Sweet Beaumont Side, and Beaumont Stream!
    There is so much of gloom and ill,
That it is soothing thus to deem
    Earth bears one spot of sunshine still;

To feel that—while my hopes decline,
    And joys from life's bleak waste depart—
One bright illusion—yet—is mine,
    One changeless landscape of the heart!

IT IS SWEET ON THIS FAIR BARK.

1836.

(Written at sea—off the coast of Essex.)

It is sweet on this fair bark to lean,
    And gaze upon the emerald sea,
Whose wavelets—breaking from the green—
    Seem snow-wreaths on an April lea,
Or birds—for so will Fancy veer—
That brightly dive, and re-appear!

There's beauty on the tinted brine,
    Which is not bounded by the coast;
For yon delightful shores are thine,
    My native land, my pride, my boast,
The peerless land where Freedom smiles,
The glorious Queen of Ocean's Isles!

YOUR NAME MAY BE NOBLE.

1836.

Your name may be noble, unsullied your race
  As the course of the mountain-rill pure from its spring,
And you may have done nothing that name to disgrace,
  But you are not a Briton, if false to your KING!

You tell me of FREEDOM, I worship it too;
  Without it, my life were a valueless thing;
But I find it consistent with LOYALTY true,—
  And you are not a Briton, if false to your KING!

You tell me of ENGLAND—I'm proud of her name;
  To all that is bright in her story I cling;
But it was under Monarchs she gathered her fame,—
  And you are not a Briton, if false to your KING!

The flock may be false to the shepherd that leads it
  Each morn during summer to pasture and spring;
The child to the parent that fondles and feeds it,
  But ne'er will a Briton be false to his KING!

O LAY HIM BY HIS FATHER!

1836.

[The "father" alluded to in this elegy, was the late Thomas Anderton, of Gargrave, a gentleman universally respected.]

O LAY him by his father,
   The mourned with many tears!
Alas! we would have rather
   He had seen his father's years:
But death will often gather
   All ages to his fold—
Then lay him by his father,
   The young man by the old!

Lay the son beside the father,
   The branch beside the tree!
We will not weep!—but rather
   Say—"Rest ye peacefully,
Till God—our shepherd—gather
   His loved ones to his fold;
Then RISE—both son and father,
   The young man and the old!"

SHE IS FALLING BY GRIEF.

1836.

[On seeing the late Mrs. L——, of Seacombe, near Liverpool.]

She is falling by grief,
   Like a rose in its prime,
Ere the bloom of its leaf
   Bears a token of time,
Which wastes every minute,
   Yet not from decay,—
But a canker within it,
   That eats it away.

No fairer draws breath;
   And no purer bore name,
Till one wrong step brought death
   To her peace and her fame.
O God! *yet* to win her
   From thoughts that o'er-prey,
From the canker within her
   That eats her away!

THE VOWS THOU HAST SPOKEN.

1836.

[Set to music by Frank de Fonblanque.]

The vows thou hast spoken
   As oft as we met,
Though lightsomely broken,
   Thou ne'er shalt forget;
But fly where thou wilt,
   Thou shalt bear with thee still
A feeling of guilt,
   And a presage of ill!

The mild moon on high
   Shall thy falsehood upbraid,
For she looked from the sky
   When the last vow was made.
The morn with its light
   Shall remind thee of me,
And my wrongs shall be blight
   On the day, and on thee!

Another may hearken
   Thy suit with a smile,
And I may not darken
   Thy hopes for a while;

But, far from thee never,
   I'll mix with thy kiss—
Intruding for ever
   Between thee and bliss!

Deem not I'd inflict
   All this woe upon thee;
Nor believe I predict
   What I gladly would see.
O! it will not abate, love,
   One sorrow of mine,
To know that a fate, love,
   Yet darker is thine!

THE MUSIC OF ANOTHER SPRING.

1836.

(Written during sickness.)

The music of another spring
   I hear, that thought not to have heard;
And seems it as no bird on wing
   Sung ever like yon early bird!

Amid the silence of the morn,
   In these sweet notes, that thrill my heart,
A hope is to my bosom born—
   I shall not—yet—from earth depart!

Fair earth—when spring-flowers round me bloom!
   Sweet time—when spring-birds round me sing!
O! but the grave's a thought of gloom,
   When all the land is gay with spring.

I SAW HER IN THE VIOLET TIME.

1837.

(On hearing of the death of Miss Hogarth—second daughter of George Hogarth, Esq., and sister-in-law of Charles Dickens—whom I had seen in high health the year before. It has been often copied and circulated.)

I saw her in the violet time,
   When bees are on the wing,
And then she stood in maiden prime—
   The fairest flower of spring!
Her glances, as the falcon's bright,
   Had archness in their ray;
Her motion and her heart were light
   As linnet's on the spray!

'Tis come again, the violet time,
  When flits the mountain bee;
And others stand in maiden prime,
  But where—O! where is *She ?*
Alas! the linnet now may sing
  Beside her early tomb!
Alas! the fairest flower of spring
  Hath perished in its bloom!

But no, but no! That maiden now,
  Immortal and serene,
Wears glory on her noble brow
  That " eye hath never seen!"
That flower, too soft for this world's air,
  Transplanted in its prime,
Blooms now where it is always fair,
  And always violet time!

THE HILLS OF MY BIRTH-PLACE.

1837.

[On revisiting my native county.]

The hills of my birth-place I gazed on once more!
And Cheviot—their Monarch—sublime as of yore,
With the snow for his mantle, the cloud for his crown,
On the white vales beneath him looked royally down!
How my eyes grasped his bulk, till they filled, and grew dim!
How I drank every breeze that was wafted from Him!

That moment of feeling, so painfully dear,
Which thus to my eyes sent the heart-gushing tear,
—A moment collecting and pouring the whole
Of the Past in a torrent at once on my soul—
As I stood in abstraction, absorbed, and alone,
I would not have changed for the pomp of a throne!

The torrent subsides when its sources are drained;
The ocean rolls back when its height is attained;
And feeling, in bosoms that years cannot dull,
Must ebb from the heart when its channels are full.

Mine ebbed, but 'twas soon to flow faster—for yet
There were scenes to be viewed, there were friends to be met!

The warm hearts of Wansbeck, how warm were they still!
How bright were the faces by Glen and by Till!
My Beaumont—I saw but her mountains of snow,
But knew that her broomy stream murmured below!
And Tweed—although Winter was curbing its speed,
No *ice* chilled the welcome I met with on Tweed!

Shall Roddam be passed? Ah! in that dearest spot,
Though I cannot forget, I am all but forgot!
Still, she has her old dell, and she has her old stream,
And a fairer* to haunt them than e'er blessed my dream;
And proudly I ween that my fame shall be there,
All fresh in her greenwoods—while greenwoods are fair!

Ay, my fame may be there; but O! never again
Shall I con, in her greenwoods, the rapturous strain!
For me each dear river all vainly will pour;
Old Cheviot himself I shall visit no more;
And the loved friends that dwell by those mountains and streams,
Henceforward, alas, will but people my dreams!

* The "fairer to haunt them" was the lady whose death is lamented in the succeeding Poem

THOUGH ALMOST TWENTY YEARS.

1837.

(On the death of Mrs. Roddam of Roddam. She was one of those beings described by Moore, as

. . . . " too lovely to remain,
Creatures of light we never see again !")

Though almost twenty years have passed
  Since I in Roddam "loved and sung"—
Though fame attends the lyre at last
  That first amid her woodlands rung—
My heart and soul are still the same;
  No scene of hers can I forget;
In spite of distance, time, and fame,
  My sweetest thoughts are Roddam's yet!

Where winds a glen and purls a rill,
  To her my fancy back they take;
Where frowns a crag and towers a hill,
  I love them for old Cheviot's sake!
The birds I hear, the flowers I see,
  Have charms that not to *them* belong—
These speak of Roddam's bloom to me,
  And those of Roddam's woodland song!

Alas, alas, for Roddam now!
    Alas for Roddam's lord the most!
Of shadowy brake and sunny brow
    The brightest, dearest charm is lost!
Low is the Lady of the Hall,
    Whom I beheld so lately there,
The loveliest and the best of all
    That ever graced the scenery fair!

I gazed, and thought——for poets build
    Most gorgeous castles on the cloud,
And with the rays of Fancy gild
    Triumphal arch and turret proud—
I thought how she, with kind regard,
    Might give old hopes again to bloom,
Might patronise her House's Bard:
    She sleeps within her House's Tomb!

Green o'er that Tomb already grow
    The laurels due to valiant deed;
A gentler wreath we mingle now
    As Beauty's and as Virtue's meed.
We bring each bloom from Roddam Dell
    That scents its depth, or gems its verge,
And bid the LYRE OF RODDAM swell
    To ring the FLOWER OF RODDAM's dirge.

THE UNION WORKHOUSE.

1837.

(Written in a desponding mood. The names are those of my children, most of whom are now beyond the reach of want and of workhouse tyranny! I cannot resist saying that the Right Honourable Matthew Talbot Baines was the first Minister who, by his humane and enlightened management, rendered the New Poor Law Act TOLERABLE to the English people.)

A House they've built on yonder slope
   Huge, grim, and prison-like, dull!
With grated walls that shut out Hope,
   And cells of wretched paupers full.
And they, if we for help should call,
   Will thither take and lodge us thus;
But, ELLEN, no! Their prison wall,
   I swear it, was not built for us!

We've lived together fourteen years;
   Three boys and four sweet girls are ours;
Our life hath had its hopes and fears,
   Its autumn blights, its summer flowers;
But ever with determined front,
   And heart that scorned in ill to bow,
Have we sustained Misfortune's brunt:
   We never quailed—nor will we now!

Our eldest hope—our Sally—she
   Who steals from e'en her play to books;
O God! in yon Bastile to see
   The sweetness of her modest looks!
And Esty, who hath little mind
   For books when there is time to play,
Her little heart would burst to find
   The same dull prison every day!

His father's picture, too, my Bob,
   My *double* both in head and heart—
And Bill, whom it were sin to rob
   Of his red cheek and emulous part—
And Fanny with her craftiness—
   And Jack who screams so very *low*—
Shall they put on their *prison-dress*?
   My dear—my dear—THEY SHALL NOT GO!

They shall not go—to pine apart,
   Forgetting kindredship and home;
To lose each impulse of the heart
   That binds us wheresoe'er we roam!
And we, whom GOD and LOVE made one,
   Whom MAN and LAW would disunite,
We will not, Famine's death to shun,
   Sleep there, or wake, a single night!

Still is their act—in something—*mild*:
   Though *I* no more must share your rest,
They would *permit* your *infant child*
   To—*tug* at an *exhausted breast!*

And Jack would cease, poor boy! to scream,
  Awed by some keeper's rod and threat;
While, sunk in cribs, the rest would dream
  Of days—too well remembered yet!

Away! on ENGLAND's soil we stand;
  Our means have, erst, supplied the poor
We *have* claims on our father-land :—
  No, no—that right is ours no more!
But we will die a Beggar's death,
  Rather than pass their hated wall!
On some free hill breathe out our breath—
  One nameless grave receiving all!

O FADED LEAF.

1837.

O FADED leaf! O faded heart!
  The summer hue of both is gone!
The storms of *fate* may do their part,
  The storms of *winter* ravage on!
The heart—the leaf—have felt the worst;
  No further blight can either know;
And—all unfeared—shall o'er them burst
  The future wind, the future woe?

Unlike the leaf in June's caress!
Unlike the heart when sorrow-free!—
But yet there springs from *hopelessness*
A stern, defying energy!
For—the worst known, and *scorned* the worst,
The man hath nought to fear below,
And asks not—recks not—*when* shall burst
The future wind, the future woe!

THE ROSE OF THE ISLES.

1837.

(This song was written on the occasion of Her Majesty's accession to the throne. Those who, like the author, are old enough to remember the late Princess Charlotte, will feel the compliment implied in the allusion to HER. A younger generation cannot.)

The Crown that encircles VICTORIA's brow,
  Transmitted through ages of fame,
To its claims on our love adds a sweeter one now,
  Derived from her sex and her name.
And the Sceptre she wields in her delicate hand,
  As she stands in the sunshine of smiles,
Hath a spell to array all the Might of the Land
  Around the fair Rose of the Isles!

Not a word of division shall burthen our breath,
    Of the parties or views we prefer;
Howe'er we may differ in feeling or faith,
    We are one—in devotion to Her!
Our Charlotte in all but her sadness of doom,
    May she live in the sunshine of smiles!
And never may sorrow-blight fall on the bloom
    Of the beautiful Rose of the Isles!

I WAS BORN IN A COT.

1837.

I was born in a Cot, and in one I may die;
    So lived and so perished my fathers obscure;
But no Peer of his lineage is prouder than I,
    For my fathers were honest, and loyal, and poor!

I envy not—covet not—title and sway;
    Yet 'tis pleasant to think that to all they are free,
That—thanks to the laws of my country! the way
    To her honours is open—ay, even to *me*.

I'm content to be part of society's *root*,
    To find that the branches which over us wave,
Derive from us foliage, blossom, and fruit,—
    And give us again all the strength that we gave.

And never, when clamour and menace are loud
    Against all that is noble, and all that is high,
Will I lend my voice to the cry of the crowd—
    I know the result of that reasonless cry!

I know that the lightning their madness would launch,
    Though meant but to injure the *loftiest shoots*,
Conducted that instant from twig and from branch,
    Would glance to, and shiver the trunk to *the roots!*

AN ENGLISHMAN'S WIFE.

1838.

(Written for a Bazaar Volume, dedicated to the late Queen Adelaide.)

The merry bells ring, and the merry boys shout,
    The matrons are gazing from window and door;
For a blithe wedding train the old Church hath poured out,
    And the green lane is crowded behind and before.

A fair Village Maiden hath promised to-day,
   To love and to cherish her Chosen through life;
And she walks by his side in her bridal array,
   To be from this moment an Englishman's Wife.

And O! if he knows it, a treasure he gains
   To which all the gems of Golconda are dim,
A counsellor kind, who in pleasures or pains,
   Will think for his welfare, exist but for him!
His children to train " in the way they should go,"
   To ward from his dwelling the entrance of strife,
To soothe him in anger, to solace in woe,
   Is the duty—the boast—of an Englishman's Wife!

Scarce heeded the light of a long sunny day,
   We love, when the sky is o'erclouded, to mark
A sun-burst on hill or on shaded vale play—
   A type of her love when his atmosphere's dark!
Her smile, in success which unheeded may beam,
   Will shine like that sun-burst when sorrows are rife,
Ay, pour round his death-bed itself a bright gleam!—
   For true to the last is an Englishman's Wife.

It is so in the cottage; and who can forget
   How deeply 'twas so in the Palace of late,
When, by the sad couch of her dying lord set,
   QUEEN ADELAIDE's watchfulness sweetened his fate?

Unwearied and sleepless—her task to fulfil,
  She sat and she soothed the last tremours of life;
And her love for our WILLIAM endears to us still
  That MODEL REVERED of an Englishman's Wife!

I BLAME THEE NOT, WORLD!

1839.

I BLAME thee not, World! that thy judgments refuse me
  The laureate wreath I have coveted long;
I have rather to thank the kind hearts that excuse me
  The times I have teased them with efforts in song.
The vision that lured me of Glory's effulgence
  Hath passed—like the bow from the cloud of the shower;
I find, after years of self-cheating indulgence,
  That the *wish* to be great I mistook for the *power*.
Then adieu to the hope, to my bosom so pleasing,
  Of being remembered and talked of when gone;
And adieu to the hope, more ambitious, of seizing
  The mind of the future, and moulding its tone!

Adieu to those fond aspirations, but never—
    While breath is within me—farewell to the Muse!
It were easier to turn from its channel yon river,
    Than me from the course that she taught me to choose.
I must still feel the changes of sky and of season,
    Be alive, like the birds, to each impulse they bring,
And, heard or *not* heard by the children of reason,
    Must at times, like those wild-birds, full-heartedly sing!
But adieu to the hope, to my bosom so pleasing,
    Of being remembered and talked of when gone;
And adieu to the hope, more ambitious, of seizing
    The mind of the future, and moulding its tone!

Perchance with myself lies the blame of bereavement
    Of the long-cherished dream of celebrity won:
Like the birds I have lived, and no worthy achievement,
    They say, without care—without labour—is done.
Hence in song, as in life, I too nearly resemble
    The light-hearted lyrists that sing in the glen,
Whose note, though it *may* bid the young bosom tremble,
    Wants the bold trumpet-tone that electrifies MEN.
Then adieu to the hope, to my bosom so pleasing,
    Of being remembered and talked of when gone;
And adieu to the hope, more ambitious, of seizing
    The mind of the future, and moulding its tone!"

DEAR HUDSON.

1840.

Dear Hudson, a winter of time has gone by
    Since last we were seated together;
But my soul never shrunk for the scowl of the sky,
    And it still bids defiance to weather!
But why should I *hint* at my griefs, 'mid the light
    That from wine and true friendship we borrow?
We wont have a word but of pleasure to-night—
    We can talk of our troubles to-morrow.

What's the want men so shun, or the wealth they so crave,
    That a care about either should bind us?
A good name is the thing, which, surviving the grave,
    Shall leave its long perfume behind us.
One hour—be futurity gloomy or bright—
    This hour shall be sacred from sorrow;
We wont have a word but of pleasure to-night—
    We can talk of our troubles to-morrow.

INGLEBORO' CAVE.

1840.

(This wonderful subterranean vault—or rather succession of irregular vaults, is but poorly described in the following stanzas. It was then a recent discovery. It is the property of James William Farrer, Esq., of Ingleboro' Hall.)

Lover of Nature! whose feet have pervaded
    The wildest recesses where verdure has birth,
And whose eyes have beheld, from these mountains unshaded,
    The grandeur of ocean, the beauty of earth,
Deem not, though thy pleasures be pure and abiding
    That thou hast exhausted the whole she e'er gave;
Go, enter yon rock, whence the waters are gliding,
    And witness the wonders she works in the cave:

Go then, and *alone*, wouldst thou feel the scene rightly,
    The Poet, invisibly joining thy side,
Shall talk with thy soul, shall be moral or sprightly,
    And summon his spirits to light thee and guide!
Look up! the green day-light yet blends with the lustres
    Sprite-furnished, and gleaming along the dark wave;
Smooth rock hung with pendants like icicle-clusters—
    What ceiling can vie with the roof of the Cave?

But on!—The day fades; and the lights, borne before
   us,
  The brighter appear, and the richer by far;
For see them beneath us, beside us, and o'er us,
  Reflected from diamond, water, and spar!
If splendour thou lovest, 'tis here in profusion,
  More pure than in courts, for it doth not deprave;
And shouldst thou point out that the whole is illusion,
  I ask, is illusion confined to the Cave?

On, on!—The lights pause. Is yon black rock the
   ending?
  No, no; thou hast farther, and fairer, to view;
So, follow we must where the elf-lights—descending,
  Half show a low vault. Don't they burn a bit *blue?*
Start not! there's no ghost, I assure you, to fear, sir;
  But stoop—lower yet—if thy head thou wouldst
   save:
Pride sometimes gets checked in his onward career, sir,
  And *Humility's* well in the world, and the Cave.

But hark! there is music! All fairy-like stealing,
  It comes on the ear, as from distance it came:
'Tis Nature's own harmony, fitfully pealing,
  And this for her Palace, the Goddess may claim.
Look round! 'tis enchantment! surpassing whatever
  The tales of the East on young fancies engrave;
So, now for description, my friend, if thou'rt clever—
  Reflect me in song this State-room of the Cave.

What song shall reflect it?—A gem-studded ceiling,
   On columns of crystal appearing to lean ;
Sides flashing with brilliants ; the wide floor reveal-
    ing
   A pure water-mirror that doubles the scene ;—
Away! 'tis prosaic, where all should be sparkling,
   And rugged, where Music should breathe through
    the stave ;
But see! my torch-bearers have left us, and—darkling
   —We follow the light as it winds up the Cave.

Then on!—We are now at the roots of the mountain,
   Where Nature, as knowing the pressure, has
    thrown
A bold massive arch o'er the line of the fountain,
   An arch *à la Gothic*—ere Gothic was known !
Here rest we before—into day-light returning—
   We return, too, to cares and to topics more grave :
And mixing a bowl while the elf-lights are burning,
   Let us drink to the health of the lord of the Cave.

SHE SHALL NOT DIE.

1841.

[On the death of Mrs. Hudson, wife of the gentleman to whom a preceding song is addressed.]

"She shall not die—as thousands die—
  To be forgot ere long;
The *poet's friend* shall claim a sigh
  While lives the *poet's song!*"

Such was the inward vow I made,
  When o'er my hour of mirth
The tidings flashed, that cold was laid
  The kindest heart on earth.

Then winter wrapped the land in snow;
  The summer decks it now;
Yet unawaked one note of woe,
  And unfulfilled my vow.

And ah! unless the poet could
  Take all of sweet and fair
That summer sheds by vale and wood,
  And all the music there—

Could take from flowers their fairest hues,
    Their sweetest notes from birds,
And by some magic skill transfuse
    The whole into his words—

How should he hope, in phrases meet,
    His tribute to prefer?
Or how reflect the virtues sweet
    That lived and bloomed in HER?

Vain effort! She who sleeps below,
    Must sleep unsung as now—
Still unawaked one note of woe,
    And unfulfilled my vow.

Save for these rhymes, which, unreproved,
    May this proud boast prolong—
"HE HAD A FRIEND TOO MUCH BELOVED,
    TOO DEEPLY MOURNED, FOR SONG!"

O SPARE THE KIND HEART.

1841.

[On reading Lord Francis Egerton's address to the Electors of South Lancashire, in which he alluded to the infirm state of his health. This Nobleman, since known as the Earl of Ellesmere, has died while these sheets were in the press. The lines may now, alas! stand as a slight but sincere tribute to his memory.]

O SPARE the kind heart long to beat as it does,
   Instinct with all feelings delightful and pure!
And spare the clear head, now so needful to us,
   Who battle our birth-right to save and secure!

When the agents of Evil are active and rife,
   When Treason, or Folly, presides at the helm,
We ask thee, O Heaven! to leave us a life
   Devoted and bound to the weal of the realm!

We ask thee to leave us that something, of which
   Crowds feel the effect, though they guess not its cause,
Which, preceding his eloquence flowing and rich,
   In look and in bearing still wins, while it awes!

We ask thee to leave us that eloquence, filled
   With all that Refinement and Genius infuse—
As soft as the dew from a spring-mist distilled,
   And sweet as the harmonies breathed by the Muse—

Coming, not like a summer-stream swollen by rain,
   A torrent that fails when the shower-cloud is gone,
But a fount-supplied river, that rolls through the
   plain,
And, strong but yet gentle, in sunshine rolls on!

We ask thee to leave us that character, bright
   With virtues not drawing their lustre from birth,
But blending with that all the charm of their light,
   To brilliance of NAME adding brilliance of WORTH.

Yes! spare the kind heart long to beat as it does,
   Instinct with all feelings delightful and pure!
And spare the clear head now so needful to us,
   When battling our birth-right to save and secure!

YON LASS YE SEE.

1841.

Yon lass ye see sae lightly trip,
She has, nae doubt, a rosy lip,
And ye might, maybe, like to sip
   Its hineyed dews yere lane, lad;
But she isna like my ain wife,
My ain, ain, ain wife,
There's nane like my ain wife—
   I'll say't and say't again, lad!

Yon lassie has a bright blue e'e,
Wi glance sae pawky and sae slee,
And ye might, maybe, like to see
   Its love-blinks a' yere ain, lad;
      But she isna like, &c.

A rosier lip, a pawkier e'e
Its mine to prize, and mine to prie,
And O! a heart that's a' for me,
   For me, and me alane, lad!
      There's nane like, &c.

When blasts o' cauld misfortune blaw,
And puirtith's showers around me fa',
Her bonnie smile gleams thro' them a',
   Like sunshine in the rain, lad!
      There's nane like, &c.

And then wi' buds she's decked my bower
As bonnie as the mither-flower,
And placed wi' them, its past my power
   To say how proud and fain, lad,
I sit beside my ain wife,
My ain, ain, ain wife,
There's nane like my ain wife—
   I'll say't and say't again, lad."

THE DAY IS GANE.

1842.

[These lines allude to a freak of mine when a boy of nine years.]

The day is gane when I could keep
    Step wi' the lave by the Ha'-house fire;
The day is gane when I could sleep
    Sound as a top in barn or byre.
I'm altered noo in mind and mood;
    In loftier things I seek my joy;
I've gotten a name wad mak' some proud;—
    But the Minstrel's no the *Minstrel's Boy!*

I hate the warl's heartless mass,
    Vile, dirty dross their end and aim;
Yet I—if I erect wad pass—
    Maun steep my soul in filth like them.
For time brought luve, and luve brought care,
    And care brings meikle o' annoy:
I'd gie some coin to wear ance mair
    The lightsome heart o' the *Minstrel's Boy!*

O SING TO ME NO MODISH TUNE.

1842.

[CALDER FAIR is the name of an air which was a great favourite with the dancers in my young days.]

O SING to me no modish tune,
    But some old Scottish air, love;
And would you give my heart a boon,
    Then sing it *Calder Fair*, love?
I know that tasteful ears would scorn
A thing so simple and so worn;
But pleasant dreams to me are borne
    In the notes of Calder Fair, love!
        Then sing to me, &c.

Again I lead the village dance,
    Or join the village ring, love;
Again I mark the roguish glance
    That Peggy used to fling, love.
The reeling and the revelry,
The wooing and the witchery,
Return in all their truth to me
    When that old air you sing, love.
        Then sing to me, &c.

It throws me back the years long fled
  On Memory's mirror true, love;
The married are again unwed,
  The faded bloom anew, love;
Her stately shape my Mary shows,
And blooms my Jeanie's lip of rose;
Ay—forms that now in dust repose,
  Are passing in my view, love!
      Then sing to me, &c.

Nor while your notes those years restore,
  Need you have doubts of me, love;
I would not wish to live them o'er,
  Nor what I've been to be, love;
With pleasure, but without regret,
I see my loves in memory yet;
For all their beauties *here* are met—
  I clasp them all in *thee*, love.
      Then sing to me, &c.

A HAPPY NEW YEAR.

1842.

There was gloom, there was grief, in the year that is sped;
But 'tis gone—and *we will not speak ill of the dead*!
Many joys it has left us, in friends that are dear,
And we'll wish one another a happy new year!

Many joys it has left us ; but some it has ta'en—
There were faces we never shall look on again ;
Kind hearts ever ready to welcome and cheer,
That now cannot wish us a happy new year !

And some we must think of, the friends of our soul !
Though far they may be from our board and our bowl ;
We know they have hearts that are warm and sincere,
And we'll wish them, though absent, a happy new
    year !

For those that are with us—their glances attest
That the same tide of feeling is high in each breast ;
That one chain of kindness links all that are here,
As we wish one another a happy new year !

Then, old friend, take my hand, and be sure—when
    I clasp—
There is heart in its pulse, there is soul in its grasp !
And if you could doubt it, this truth-speaking tear
Will tell *how* I wish you a happy new year !

MUTE IS THE LYRE OF EBOR.

1842.

"We bring our years to an end, as it were a tale that is told."
PSALMS.

(On the death of John Nicholson, well known in the North as "The Airedale Poet." His life has been forcibly written by my friend John James, and prefixed to a posthumous edition of the poet's works—published for the benefit of his widow and children. Mr. James is himself distinguished by a "History of Bradford," which has been pronounced one of the very best local histories extant.)

Mute is the Lyre of Ebor! cold
    The Minstrel of the streamy Aire!
The "years" are passed, the "tale" is told
    Prepare the shroud, the grave prepare!

The tale is told—what is the tale?
    The same that still the ear hath won,
As oft as, in life's humbler vale,
    Genius hath found a wayward Son.

First comes the magic time of life,
    When Boyhood sees nor dreams of gloom;
And when within the breast are rife
    Thoughts that are made of light and bloom!

Then Youth will all its burning hopes
    Of fame and glory ne'er to die,
When manfully with fate he copes,
    And *will* not see a peril nigh.

At length he gives to public gaze
    The transcript of his glowing thought;
And vulgar marvel, high-born praise,
    Seem earnests of the meed he sought.

Now round him crowd, where'er he wends,
    His mind yet pure and undebased,
The countless troop of *talent's friends*,
    Men who affect—but have not—taste.

These bid him press to eager lips
    The double poison of their bowl—
Flatteries that weaken as he sips,
    And draughts that darken sense and soul!

O for a voice to rouse him up,
    To warn him ere too late it be,
That Frenzy mantles in the cup,
    And that its dregs are—Misery!

Days pass—years roll—the novelty
    That charmed at first, is faded now:
And men that *sought* his hour of glee,
    Repel him with an altered brow.

Where is the bard's indignant breath?
    Alas, the bard, from habits learned
Is powerless to resent; and Death
    Kindly receives him—spent and spurned!

Talk ye of FAME? O! he hath borne
    Contempt, alive; but praise him, dead!
Ay, mourn him—whom ye left to mourn!
    Give him a stone—ye gave not bread!

No more. The old, sad tale is told
    Prepare the shroud, the grave prepare;
For mute is Ebor's Lyre, and cold
    The Minstrel of the streamy Aire!

I WOULD NOT PASS FROM EARTH.

1842.

(This is the last piece of verse I composed in Craven.)

I WOULD not pass from Earth
    In the sweet spring-time,
When all fair things have birth
    In our Northland clime!
When the forest's song is new;
When the violet blooms in dew;
When the living woods are seen
In their first and freshest green;

When the laughing mead unfolds
A hue that shames the gold's;
When each hawthorn-hedge, in blow
Seems a wreath of summer snow;
When the azure river glides
Through flowers that fringe its sides,
And, crowding rich and rife,
Drink thence exulting life;—
O! I would not vanish *then*
From the world of living men!

I know that, after death,
The Soul shall draw her breath
In a purer, finer air,
And 'mid scenes surpassing fair;
But I feel—and be it said
Not profanely!—might I tread
The vales of Heaven, e'en *then*
I should dream of earth again!
So deep, here, the love-trace
Of nature and of place,
That my musings would come back
To their old and hallowed track,
Leave the pure life-waters there
For the Beaumont and the Aire!
    For beautiful is earth
      In the sweet spring-time,
    When all fair things have birth
      In our Northland clime!

POOR MARY.

1842.

["Poor Mary" was Mary Batty, of Skipton,—a fair pupil of mine.]

In spring, alas! poor Mary dies,
    Ere many springs have found her;
An early-blighted flower she lies,
    When all is blooming round her!

Yet consolation gilds the tear
    With which her fate we ponder:
She never caused a sorrow *here*,
    And ne'er will meet one *yonder*!

ABOVE THE LINE OF LAMPS.

1843.

[Written in London.]

Above the line of lamps, above
    The smoke that dims the evening air,
The Moon, whose beams I used to love,
    Is shining now as calmly fair—

I cannot doubt—as when she smiled
    Upon me in some Northern glen,
Or by some mountain vast and wild,
    Where rocks were—not rock-hearted men.

And even now on many a spot—
    Still loved, though left—she glances down;
Beheld by, but beholding not,
    My friends in hamlet and in town.

I would I were upon her sphere!
    And were with powers of vision blest,
Extensive as her beams and clear!—
    O! where would, then, my vision rest?

Not on the stars—though Mystery
    Sat 'mid their orbs, my gaze to draw!
Not on the seas—though gloriously
    Flashed thence the pomp of Night I saw!

But on the hills, and by the streams,
    Whose very names are *song* to me;
And round the homes, where fancy dreams
    Warm-hearted friends of mine may be.

On Cheviot, sung in many a lay;
    By Beaumont, named in few but mine;
By Till, that past the ruins gray
    Of Etal leads its silver line;

By Wansbeck, rippling on its course;
   By Tyne, that mirrors banks so fair;
By streamy Aire's romantic source;
   And by the Ribble—dear as Aire!

Hallowed by Friendship and the Muse,
   O'er them mine eyes would rove or rest:
For I am one who never lose
   One kind emotion of the breast.

Let the cold sons of Reason claim
   The praise of science and of art;
All art, all science, and their fame,
   Are nothing—weighed against the HEART!

IT NE'ER WAS SPAK'.

1844.

[Written in one of the fields of Roddam.]

It ne'er was spak', but aft was *look'd*;
   I ken'd it in your e'e, Jeanie;
An' for the luve to me ye bore,
   . I've often thought o' thee, Jeanie.

While faces, ance preferr'd to thine,
    I willingly forget, Jeanie;
Thy sonsie look o' unsought luve,
    I mind and prize it yet, Jeanie!

An' now I'm in the field we reap'd,
    An' sigh to think ye're gane, Jeanie;
For finer form there might ha been—
    But kinder heart was nane, Jeanie!

THE BONNIE PINK FLOWER.

1844.

[The hill alluded to in the following lines is the Lanton Hill so often mentioned. I saw the flower and wrote the song in 1844. It has been set to Music by Mr. Waller, with accompaniments by Thirlwall.]

I cam to the hill whare a boy I had wandered
    An' high beat my heart when I traced it again!—
As up its steep side—now an auld man—I dandered,
    I stopp'd whare a bonnie Pink blossom'd its lane.
It seem'd a wee star lighted up amang heather!
    My first thought said—"Pu' it, an' bring it away,"
But a tenderer pleaded—"How soon it wad wither!
    O! leave it to bloom on its ain native brae!

" For wha kens," pled the Thought, " but this bonnie
     flower bloomin',
  May hae some kin' o' feelin' or sense o' its ain ?
It 'ill change wi' the lift, be it smilin' or gloomin',
  Exult in the sunshine, an' droop in the rain.
An' wha kens that it hasna some pleasure in gi'ein'
  Its bloom to the e'e an' its sweets to the day ?
That it hasna a secret an' sweet sense o' *bein'* ?"—
  Sae I left it to bloom on its ain native brae !

Wad the young man but learn frae this simple
     narration,
  When he meets wi' a bonnie lass bloomin' her lane,
To think—that tho' poor, an' tho' lowly in station,
  The lass has a *heart* he may please, or may pain !
Then, if he can mak' her a wife, let him tak' her,
  An' bear her in joy an' in triumph away !
But O ! if he canna—beguile her he manna,
  But leave her to bloom on her ain native brae !

MONY AULD FRIEN'S.

1844.

(The gentleman whose death called forth these lines—the "Dear Hudson" of a very different song in this collection—was, without one exception, the best man I ever knew. His enthusiastic friendship for myself, his disinterested zeal for my reputation and success—I shall never forget. Nor has he all died! On my last visit to Yorkshire, I found his SPIRIT still animating his friends, and meeting me at every turn, with the welcome of the years that are past.

"Alas, how different—yet how like the same!")

Mony auld frien's to Town come, in kindness, to me,
Wi' the heart in the hand, an' the soul in the e'e;
An' blithely I meet them, as aft as they ca';
But there's ane that comes never—the dearest of a'!

There's aften some failin' where maist ane wad lean;
Some mickle 'll praise when but little they mean.
You felt his heart beat in ilk word *he* let fa';
But that kind ane comes never—the dearest of a'!

It isna the distance—that soon wad be pass'd;
Its nae fit o' cauldness—that short while wad last;
Its the stern grip o' Death that keeps Hudson awa',
An' he will come never—the dearest of a'!

My ain day is closin', and I, too, maun dee;
I scarce care how soon—if wi' him I may be!
For nane but guid fellows around him 'ill draw,
And be they a' monarchs, he's King o' them a'!

O LET US BE FRIENDLY?

1845.

(Written for an annual dinner party, chiefly composed of certain officials of the Houses of Parliament.)

O LET us be friendly! since brief is life's day,
And seldom undimmed by some trouble its ray,
'Twere folly in rancour or strife to employ
One moment that might be devoted to joy.
Impressed with this truth are the hearts that meet here,
For a banquet of friendship and mirth once a year;
And no strife shall intrude, and no rancour ensue,
For "Be friendly" 's the word when I'm dining with You.

At home we have cares—but we leave them to-day;
In the world there is business—'tis not in our way;
Our business goes on, when our joys are improving,
And our care is, to see that the bottles keep moving!
The Queen, be she happy!—we're happy as she;
The Lords, be they wise—are they wiser than we?
And as for the Commons, I hold it quite true,
I am not *of* the Commons when dining with You!

Then fill a round bumper, and each, in his place,
Drink with me—TO THE WEAL OF THE WHOLE HUMAN
   RACE!
Whatever his colour, his clime, or his creed,
Be he savage or civilised, fettered or freed,
Each man upon us hath the claim of a brother!
And if you can be touched by the woes of another,
You will pledge me with feelings befitting and due,
Nor allow them to part—when I've parted from You!

WE OFTEN LAUGHED AT FANNY.

1846.

We often laughed at Fanny,
  But we loved her while we laughed;
She was so odd a mixture
  Of simplicity and craft.
Whate'er she thought she uttered,
  And her words—she "reckon'd nou't"
Of the fine flash talk of London—
  Hers was Yorkshire out and out!

While her little schemes of cunning,
  Which she thought so veiled, were still
As obvious as the channel
  Of the purest mountain rill.
Thus her heart being good and gentle,
  And transparent all her craft,
We often laughed at Fanny,
  But we loved her while we laughed!

A short life was my Fanny's,
  And slight the warning given!
But her sins were those of childhood,
  And her spirit is in Heaven.
All through her words, when dying,
  Ran a vein of solemn thought;
And we felt how *wise* was Fanny,—
  We had laughed more than we ought.
Yet even in those moments
  Came out a phrase, a word,
That reminded us of periods
  When the same with mirth we heard.
And we oft recall her sayings,
  Her playfulness and craft;
But now—'tis odd—we weep the most
  At what the most we laughed!

MY WILLIAM.

1846.

My William died in London,
  In London broad and brave;
His little life was but a drop
  Dashed from her mighty wave!
And few there were that mourned my boy,
  When he went to his grave.

Few mourned—and when we laid him
  In his earth-bed cold and low,
No hireling Mute, I said, should stand
  In mimicry of woe;
But genuine tears, from eyes he loved,
  Flowed forth—as still they flow.

I thought—but that was weakness—
  I had rather seen him laid
In the distant, rural, green churchyard
  Near which a child he played,
With daisies o'er the turf to bloom,
  And no dull walls to shade.

How shall we e'er forget him?
 His eye, instinct with light—
His cheek's fair bloom, which Death itself
 Found it most hard to blight—
His little manly bearing—all
 That made our cottage bright!

Above a boy ambitious,
 To learn, to work, to *rise*—
Beyond his years considerate,
 And *ominously* wise—
O how I prized him! *Now*, it seems
 That *half* I did not prize.

O London! fatal London!
 How proud to come was I!
How proud was *he*! how proud were all!
 And all have come—to die!
Pass on, sad years! and close the tale
 With its best words—" HERE LIE"——

THE CHAIN IS BROKEN, FATHER.

1847.

[Supposed to be addressed to her father by Mrs. D——, (who had been unhappily married,) on the death of her mother.]

The chain is broken, Father,
   That bound together *three;*
The middle link is taken;—
   But thou art left to me,
And I to thee, my Father!
   And here I promise thee,
That ne'er was truer Daughter found,
   Than thou shalt find in me!

I have no tie to life, Father;
   Save thee, I have not one!
I bear indeed the name of wife,
   But husband I have none.
I name not this regretfully—
   All that is over now—
I name it but to let thee see
   That my sole tie art Thou!

And I will tend thee, Father,
   As long as I have breath;
And if it please my Mother's God,
   I'll tend thy bed of death.
Then, the last tie dissevered,
   I'll follow her and thee,
Where Love shall join the links again
   That bound together *three!*

SLEEP, MY MARY!

1847.

[Music by Thirlwall.]

Sleep, my Mary! sleep, my Mary!
   Sleep, though darksome be thy bed;
Sleep my Mary! sleep, my Mary!
   Sleep, though round thee lie the dead!
Sleep!—To *this* bed comes not nigh
   Tortured night, or troubled day;
Fearless sleep, the dead that lie
   Round thee—O how harmless they!

Sleep, my Mary! sleep, my Mary!
   Dream not thou art left alone—
Listen, Mary! listen, Mary!
   Well was once my footstep known!—
Hush!—That sob was much too loud;
   Glad I am the grave is deep!
It would pain her in her shroud,
   Could she hear her father weep!

Sleep, my Mary! sleep, my Mary!
   Dead thou art not—scarce *removed*;
Still, my Mary! still, my Mary!
   Thou art living, thou art loved!
Living still—at least to me,
   Still before my inward eye;
Loved—as nothing else can be!
   Loved—till life and memory die!

'TIS SWEET TO ESCAPE.

1847.

[Music by the same.]

'Tis sweet to escape from the noise of the city,
   And spend one free day with a few we hold dear,
Who—all of them pleasant, and some of them witty,
   Are sure to make *that* day the gem of the year.

The Thames that rolls by with its freightage of
     treasure,
   Must ebb—while we sit—in its changeful career;
But no ebb shall take place in our spring-tide of
     pleasure,
   Till the sun has gone down on this gem of the year!

If the days we have passed had their trouble or sorrow,
   If the heart had its pang, and the eye had its tear,
Sad thought may return with the gloom of to-morrow;
   Such thought shall not sully this gem of the year!

'Tis a banquet of Friendship, which after-reflection
   The deeper shall hallow, the more shall endear;
For long shall come back on each pleased recollection
   The beauty and light of this gem of the year!

AT PARKER'S TOMB.

1848.

[I knew the late Mr. Parker, of the Iff, in the West-Riding of Yorkshire, well. He deserved every word of the character I have given him in the Epitaph.]

At Parker's Tomb—exulting—say:
    He from the right ne'er swerved,
But, faithfully and well, "his day
    And generation" served.

Unwarped by censure or applause;
    Still firm, however tried;
The world's amount of virtue was
    Diminished when he died!

His death was mourned by friends untold,
    And e'en his foes confess,
That now the Queen's dominions hold
    One honest man the less.

MY BARK IS ON THE TYNE.
1849.

(Founded on an old Northumbrian song, of which I never heard more than the tune and chorus:
" . . . . Till the tide come in, till the tide come in,
We'll kiss a bonny lassie till the tide come in."
Set to music by Alicia Bennett.)

My bark is on the Tyne, and the wind blows fair;
The tide is rising fast, and I've little time to spare;
But, before the latest moment, to part would be a sin!
So we'll kiss, my bonny Mary, till the tide come in.
Till the tide come in, till the tide come in,
We'll kiss, my bonny Mary, till the tide come in.

But why that filling eye, and that pale drooping brow?
I cannot bear those sighs, love! I pray suppress them now.
Let all without seem pleasure, though all be sad within,
And we'll kiss, my bonny Mary, till the tide come in.
   Till the tide come in, &c.

I thank thee for that smile, it is sunshine to me;
And I'll keep it in my heart when I'm far away at sea;
It will lighten on my watch when the lonely hours begin!
So we'll kiss, my bonny Mary, till the tide come in.
   Till the tide come in, &c.

It will lighten on my watch, like a moonbeam on
    deck ;
It will shine if there be battle, it will gleam if there
    be wreck ;
It will nerve my soul in danger, an honoured name
    to win !
So we'll kiss, my bonny Mary, till the tide come in.
        Till the tide come in, &c.

Again that eye is filled ! Well, unblamed it now
    must be ;
But weep not long, my dearest ; and breathe oft a
    prayer for me !
That prayer shall safe return me from the storm's or
    battle's din,
To woo my bonny Mary till the tide come in !
        Till the tide come in, &c.

O SCORN NOT THE PLOUGH.

1849.

O scorn not the Plough! which for ages hath been
   The boast of this Isle of the Free;
And for ages to come, when our tombstones are green,
   Our posterity's boast let it be.
Our cottons and silks we might give to the moth,
   Nor be much the worse off, you'll allow;
The loom, after all, can but furnish his *Cloth*,
   The *Man* is sustained by the Plough!

It was well with our sires when their wives spun the fleece
   That at church and at market they wore;
When the loom—still domestic—was clicking in peace
   On the flags of the cottager's floor.
And though manners have changed, yet let worst come to worst,
   We could live as they lived, even now;
For garb is but second, food ever is first,
   And our food is produced by the Plough!

When England waged war—as again she may do,
    And conquered as conquer she will,
Whence came the brave bands that, on red Waterloo,
    Kept her soil the free soil it is still?
All fresh from the country—not pale from the towns,
    They marched, as they still would, I trow;
The fine healthy men of the dales and the downs,
    The broad-shouldered sons of the Plough!

THE SEASONS IN PASSING.

1849.

The seasons, in passing, one sweet moral bring,
    And well—if he marked it—would man do;
"Spread pleasure—like *me*," is the language of Spring,
    "Make all hearts as glad as you can do!"

The Summer but varies it: "Make each heart glad,
    Treat all with the warmth of affection;
My sun shines alike on the good and the bad,
    And shall *you* dare to think of selection?"

The Autumn repeats it : " My stores are for *all ;*
    But should one, in the scramble, get favour,
Let him share it with those to whom little may fall,
    And what's left will have all the more savour !"

And Winter affirms it—while shaking the door,
    And binding the stream with his fetter :
" Keep the cold that I bring, from the hearths of the poor,
    And your own will burn brighter and better !"

So speaks every Season that comes and departs,
    To the bosoms of all men appealing—
Alas, that it touches so few of our hearts !
    That so many continue unfeeling !

What a world it would be, if—less mindful of pelf—
    We esteemed every neighbour a brother ;
And if each, while he did a bit good for himself,
    Did a little bit, too, for another !

IN YOUTH OUR FATHERS.

1849.

(For Her Majesty's birth-day.)

In youth, our fathers sought the wood,
    Or climbed the hill at dawning gray;
Our mothers, in their maidenhood,
    Donned their best garb to greet the May.
And though old rites have passed away,
    The May is still with honour seen—
We love the Month that brings the day,
    The natal day of England's Queen.

Our fathers twined the blossomed bough
    To deck their chosen Queen of May;
To ours, their love Three Kingdoms vow,
    An Empire's millions homage pay!
Their May-Queen reigned a single day,
    Then passed, unnoticed, o'er the green;
Through all the year we own the sway,
    And bless the rule of England's Queen!

May brings, at eve, the loveliest star,
  At eve, the moon of softest ray;
In May, the night's the fairest far,
  The sweetest morning breaks—in May.
Then brightest blooms the woodland spray,
  Then purest lies the dew-drop sheen—
As Nature's self would grace the day
  That graced the world with England's Queen!

MY BLESSING ON.

1851.

(In the farm-house of Threestoneburn, among the Cheviots, I have seen three generations of the same family, and have spent many happy hours with all of them.

My blessing on yonder wild mountains,
  On yonder wild valley between,
And on the sweet cot and its fountains,
  The sweetest by wanderer seen!
How gladly—the world's weary ranger—
  My days in that cot could I spend,
Whose door ne'er was barred on a stranger,
  Whose bed—ne'er denied to a friend!

The morn o'er the moorland was shining,
    A morn without one streak of gloom—
'Twas splendour with beauty combining,
    The blending of sunshine and bloom!
And the cot had each spell—when I found it,
    The heart and the fancy to win;
For all mountain charms were around it,
    And all mountain virtues within!

O sweet was the flower of the heather,
    As it bloomed in the sun and the dew;
But a sweeter flower there *he* may gather,
    Who goes with a pure hand and true!
For that cot has some lovelier blossoms
    Than even the heather supplies—
The father's good heart in their bosoms,
    The mother's kind glance in their eyes!

WHO WOULD NOT BE PROUD OF OLD ENGLAND?

1853.

Who would not be proud of old England,
    With her great heart both tender and strong?
Aye ready to soften at sorrow,
    Aye ready to kindle at wrong!

To her friends a tall rock of the desert,
    Whose fount with sweet water o'erflows;
An Etna in red-hot eruption,
    And darting round death—to her foes.

Those rights which the nations still sigh for,
    She, ages ago, made her own:
No slave she permits in her borders,
    No tyrant she brooks on her throne!

Supreme on her own mighty Island,
    With the sea for her subject, she stands;
And millions obey her and love her,
    Who never set foot on her sands!

We are loath to think Liberty mortal—
    Undying we hold her to be;
Yet Liberty's life is bound up with
    The life of this Queen of the sea!

INTRODUCTION TO GUTHRUM THE DANE.

TO SIR WALTER SCOTT.

Soul of the Last and Mightiest
Of all the Minstrels—be thou blest!
For that thou hast bequeathed to me
A great and glorious Legacy,
Such as no other single mind—
Save Shakspeare's—ever left behind!
One, not of earth, or earth-born gold,
In acres broad, or sums untold,
Which may by heirs be wasted, may
By lawless force be swept away,
Or meanly filched by legal stealth;
But a bequest of Mental Wealth!
Left, not to me alone, although
As much my own as if 'twere so;
And yet, high thanks to art divine,
As much the world's as it is mine:
E'en like the air, or like the sun,
Enjoyed by all, engrossed by none;
Diffused, unspent, entire, though shared—
All undiminished, unimpaired;
Ordained to rouse emotions high,
And charm—till England's language die!

O! when at first I saw the Tale
Which tells of the redoubted Gael,[1]
And of the bard[2] whose harp would wake
To soothe the Lady of the Lake,
I did not *read*—That term were weak
The process of the hour to speak.
Page after page, thy words of flame
To me—without a medium—came!
The instant glanced at, glanced the whole
Not on my *sight*, but on my *soul!*
And, thus daguerreotyped, each line
Will there remain while life is mine!
I deemed that lay the sweetest far
That ever sung of love and war;
And vowed that, ere my dying day,
I would attempt such lovely lay.
But I was young, and had forgot
How different were from thine, O Scott!
My genius, and my earthly lot.

What though my ear, in boyhood's time,
Delighted, drank the flowing rhyme?
Though then, like Pope, no fool to fame,
" I lisped in numbers," for they came,
And waked, uncensured, unapproved,
An echo of the strain I loved?
And what though, in maturer days,
With none to judge, and few to praise,

Survived and ruled the impulse strong,
And my heart lived and moved in song?
Still—poor, unfriended, and untaught,
A Cyclops in my Cave of Thought,
Long sought I round, ere glimpse of day
Consoled me with its entering ray.
At length it came! and then I tried
To wake my Harp in lonely pride.

My Harp was made from stunted tree,
The growth of Glendale's barest lea;[3]
Yet fresh as prouder stems it grew,
And drank, with leaf as green, the dew—
Bright showers, from Till or Beaumont shed,
Its roots with needful moisture fed;
Gay birds, Northumbrian skies that wing,
Amid its branches loved to sing;
And purple Cheviot's breezy air
Kept up a life-like quivering there.
From Harp, thence rudely framed and strung,
Ah! how should strain like thine be flung?
If, moved by young ambition's dream,
I struck it to some lofty theme,
All harshly jarred its tortured chords,
As 'plaining such should be its lord's;
But all its sweetness wakened still
To lay of Northern stream or hill!
To CRAVEN's emerald dales transferred,
That simple Harp with praise was heard.

The manliest sons, the loveliest daughters,
That flourish by the Aire's young waters;
By gentle Ribble's verdant side,
And by the Wharfe's impetuous tide,
Lauded its strains. And for this cause,
While throbs my breast to kind applause—
Nay, when, beneath the turf laid low,
No kind applause my breast can know—
A *Poet's blessing*, heart-bequeathed,
O'er the domains of Craven breathed,
Shall be to every hill and plain
Like vernal dew, or summer rain,
And stay with her, while bud or bell
Decks lowland mead, or upland fell![4]

There—mindful still of thee—I strove
To frame a lay of war and love.
I roused old heroes from the urn;
Bade buried monks to day return;
And waked fair maids, whose dust had lain
Ages in lead, to bloom again;
My grateful wish to pour along
Those emerald dales the charm of song,
And do for Malham's Lake and Cave
What thou hadst done for Katrine's wave.
Not that the pride impelled me now
That had inspired my youthful vow;
I would but some *like notes* essay,
Not rashly wake a rival lay!

But years of gloom and strife came on ;
Dark omens girt the British Throne ;
The Disaffected and the Bad,
Who hopes from wild commotion had,
Gave towns to tumult and to flame,
And treason wrought—in WILLIAM's name !
That was no time, in idle lays,
To kindle feuds of other days—
I tuned my Harp to Order's cause,
And sung for Britain's King and Laws ! [5]
For party ? Ay ! but party *then*
Was led by England's greatest men—
By *Him*, [6] to save his country born,
By *Him*, [7] whom all the people mourn ;
'Twas graced by STANLEY's [8] noble name,
And vaunted that of 'gallant GRAEME.' [9]
Men—far too high, too pure, too proud,
To flatter either court or crowd ;
Men—moved by patriotic zeal,
And seeking nought but England's weal !
Dull were the head could style the man
Who followed *them*, a partisan.

Far from thy Tweed—my birth that claims—
I find myself on regal THAMES !
The swans that SPENCER loved to sing,
Before me prune the snowy wing ;
In Surrey woods, by moonlight pale,
I list to THOMSON's nightingale ; [10]

Use the same walks that COLLINS used,
And muse, where POPE himself hath mused!"¹
What wonder if the wish, that burned
So strong in youth, in age returned;
And—'mid such scenes—my Harp again
Took up the long-abandoned strain?
But ah! when of the high design
Is traced at length the closing line,
I say not—How unlike to thine!
(The forward child of youthful pride,
That bold Presumption long hath died)
But—How unlike to that which first
On my enraptured Fancy burst,
When, fresh and fair, my untried theme
Rose—like a landscape in a dream!
That landscape hath familiar grown,
And half of its romance is flown.
Thus regions new, in distance seen,
Have sunny vales of smoothest green,
And mountains which, as they ascend,
With the blue sky so softly blend,
That—giving nought of *earth* to view—
They seem to be ethereal too!
But, visited, the change is harsh;
The vales that looked so smooth, are marsh;
Brushwood and heath the hills array;
And rock and quagmire bar the way!
—— Yet round that marsh, who seek the vale,
May violet find, or primrose pale;

Yet on those hills, who choose to climb,
May meet the crow-flower or the thyme;
While e'en the rock for buds has room,
And e'en the quagmire boasts its bloom!

And, well I hope, that Northman ne'er
Will lend a cold fastidious ear,
To hear a Native Bard rehearse
In the good old heroic verse,
How, bold of heart and strong of hand,
His DANISH FATHERS won NORTHUMBERLAND.

NOTES.

1 Roderick Dhu.   2 Allan-Bane.

3 Glendale, one of the minor divisions of the county of Northumberland, takes its name from the small stream of the Glen.

4 This, and the preceding paragraph, have already appeared in the Epistle to Gourley; but to have omitted them here, would have marred the Introduction.

5 I trust that this will not be considered a too ostentatious allusion to a number of loyal and patriotic lyrics, which successively appeared in most of the leading journals of the day, and which, in their collected form, went through three editions.

6 The Duke of Wellington.   7 The late Sir Robert Peel.

8 Now the Earl of Derby.   9 Sir James Graham.

10 Thomson's fondness for the song of the nightingale is well known. He was in the habit of sitting at his open window half the summer night, entranced with its unrivalled music. The name of Collins, in my mind, is inseparably connected with that of Thomson, by his beautiful Elegy on the death of the latter.

11 I allude to Battersea, the lanes and walks of which must have been familiar to the great poet, from his frequent visits to the mansion of his friend, Lord Bolingbroke, at that place.

FAIREST OF ALL STARS.

1852.

[In memory of Sarah, my eldest daughter—the same who plucked the violet in 1825. See page 40.]

Fairest of all Stars! Star of the Even!
   See'st thou a Soul pass—fairer than thou?
Brief though the time since she left us for Heaven,
   Perhaps, in her journey, she passes thee now!
Angels she wants not to guide or attend her,
   Certain and safe is her path through the skies;
Ray as she was from the Source of all splendour,
   Back to that Source she—instinctively—flies!

Spirits will hail her; sisters and brothers
   Give to her greeting a joyful response—
O! will they talk of their father and mother's
   Death-darkened home—which was bright with
     them once?
Talk of it, blest ones! early selected!
   Memories of sadness, no sadness will bring;
Joy will seem sweeter for woes recollected,
   As Winter, remembered, adds beauty to Spring!

THE PEERAGE OF INDUSTRY.

1853.

(Written for, and recited at, the opening of the great Model Mill of Saltaire, near Bradford, where about four thousand guests, nearly three thousand of whom were Mr. Salt's own work-people, sat down to a sumptuous dinner, all in one room. The lines have been circulated wherever the English language is read—a distinction as much above their merit, as was the liberality—worthy of the " Lord of Saltaire"—with which they were acknowledged.)

To the praise of the Peerage high harps have been strung,
  By Minstrels of note and of name;
But a Peerage we have, to this moment unsung,
  And why should not *they* have their fame?
'Tis the PEERAGE OF INDUSTRY! Nobles who hold
  Their patent from Nature alone—
More genuine far than if purchased with gold,
  Or won, by mean arts, from a throne!
And of Industry's Nobles, what name should be first,
  If not *his* whose proud banquet we share?
For whom should our cheers simultaneously burst,
  If not for the Lord of Saltaire?
For this is his praise—and who merit it not,
  Deserve no good luck should overtake them—
That while making his thousands, he never forgot
  The thousands that helped him to make them!

x

The Peer who inherits an ancient estate,
    And glads many hearts with his pelf,
We honour and love; but is that man less great,
    Who founds his own fortune himself?
Who builds a town round him; sends joy to each hearth;
    Makes the workman exult 'mid his toil;
And who, while supplying the markets of Earth,
    Enriches his own beloved soil?
Such a man is a Noble, whose name should be first,
    In our heart—in our song—in our prayer!
For such should our cheers simultaneously burst,
    And such is the Lord of Saltaire!
For this is his praise—and who merit it not,
    Deserve no good luck should overtake them—
That while making his thousands, he never forgot
    The thousands that helped him to make them!

YOU HAVE HEARD.

1853.

[For the fairy tale of the Whistle, see Thorp's "Yule-tide Stories." Music by Jay.]

"You have heard," said a youth to his sweetheart who stood,
  While he sat on a corn-sheaf, at daylight's decline,
"You have heard of the Danish boy's whistle of wood—
  I wish that the Danish boy's whistle were mine!"

"And what would you do with it? Tell me!" she said,
  While an arch smile played round her beautiful face;
"I would blow it," he answered, "and then my fair maid
  Would fly to my side, and would here take her place."

"Is *that* all you wish it for? *That* may be yours
  Without any magic," the fair maiden cried;
"A favour so slight one's good nature secures!"
  And she playfully seated herself by his side.

"I would blow it again," said the youth, "and the charm
Would work so, that not even Modesty's check
Would be able to keep from my neck your fine arm!"
   She smiled, and she laid her fine arm round his neck.

"Yet once more would I blow, and the music divine
   Would bring me, the third time, an exquisite bliss—
You would lay your fair cheek to this brown one of mine,
   And your lips, stealing past it, would give me a kiss.

The maiden laughed out in her innocent glee—
   "What a fool of yourself with the whistle you'd make!
For only consider, how silly 'twould be
   To sit there and *whistle for*—what you might take!"

WE REAR NO WAR-DEFYING FLAG.

1853.

We rear no war-defying flag,
    Though armed for battle still ;
The feeble, if he like, may brag—
    The powerful never will.
The flag we rear in every breeze,
    Float where it may, or when,
Waves forth a signal o'er the seas
    Of—" Peace, Good-will to men !"

For arms, we waft across the waves
    The fruits of every clime ;
For death, the truth that cheers and saves ;
    What mission more sublime ?
For flames, we send the lights afar
    Out-flashed from press and pen ;
And for the slogans used in war,
    Cry—" Peace, Good-will to men !"

But are there States who never cease
    To hate or envy ours ?
And who esteem our wish for peace
    As proof of waning powers ?

Let them but dare the trial! High
    Shall wave our war-flag then!
And woe to those who change our cry
    Of " Peace, Good-will to men!"

BRING OUT THE OLD WAR-FLAG.

1854.

—

Bring out the old War-flag! Long, now, it has lain,
    Its folds—rich with glory—all piously furled;
And the hope of our heart was, that never again
    Should we see it float forth in the wars of the world.
For still we remembered the blood, and the tears,
    Both real—for sight, not imagined—for song,
That dimmed e'en its triumphs through many dark years,
    When it waved in the battles of Right against Wrong!

But down with regrets! or leave them to our foes,
    Whose outrage forbids us at peace to remain—
And up with it now from its honoured repose,
    'Mid the cheers of a people that cheer not in vain!

They cheer to behold it once more coming forth,
　The weak to defend from the sword of the strong;
For—true to its fame—the first flag of the North
　Will but wave in the battles of Right against Wrong!

Take, Warriors of Freedom, the flag we bestow,
　To be shortly unfurled at the trumpet's wild breath!
We give it you stainless; and Britons, we know,
　Will bring it back stainless, or clasp it in death!
But why talk of death, save of death to our foes,
　When ye meet them in conflict—too fierce to be long?
O! safe is the War-flag, confided to those
　Who fight in the battles of Right against Wrong!

SHE TRIED TO SMILE.

1855.

["The Empress endeavoured to smile, in acknowledgment of the cheers, but her feelings overcame her: she threw herself back, and gave way to a flood of tears."—Report of the attempted assassination of the French Emperor.]

She tried to smile, for she would fain
   Have so received her people's cheers;
But her heart found the effort vain,
   And it gushed o'er in copious tears.
Above the Empress, in that strife,
Arose the Woman and the Wife.

She turned to her imperiled mate
   With—who shall say what mingled pangs?—
On whose attempted life the fate
   Of Europe, at this moment, hangs—
How looked he when thus sorely proved?
He was the only one unmoved!

Heaven-raised, Heaven-shielded, there he sat,
   Impassive as the mountain rock—
A thousand storms may blaze round that,
   It stirs not at the mightiest shock.
The fountain in its breast may quiver—
Its aspect is the same for ever!

And hides not He, beneath that cold
  Calm front, a tender fountain too?
And felt he not how sweet to hold
    The empire of a bosom true?
And deemed he not each tear a gem
Worth all that grace his diadem?

O happy in this double sway
  Of heart and empire? Thou canst boast
That were the empire wrenched away,
  The heart left, there were little lost;
The heart which blesses now thy lot,
Would make a palace of a cot!

MY BLESSING ON BRADFORD.

My blessing on Bradford! though smoky it be,
No town in broad Yorkshire is dearer to me:
It is dear for the Past when full often a guest,
I sat at its board with the friends I loved best;
When wine made our many *Symposia* divine,
And the kindness was even more prized than the wine.
It is dear for the Present; for though I am thrown
In this vast and cold desert of brick and of stone,

With leagues interposed between Bradford and me—
If a hundred old friends from the country I see,
Be sure of that hundred (most ask me to dine!)
The noble Bradfordians make ninety and nine!
Then can I but love it? though dark be its wreath,
I know what is *warming* and *shining* beneath;
Its *Genius* to me is a gloom-chasing spell,
And the light of its *Friendships* doth darkness dispel.

OUR NIGHTINGALE'S FAME.

1855.

When a Knight of the old time was wounded in war,
    His lady-love flew to the field where he lay,
Had him carefully borne to some castle afar,
    And tended his sick couch by night and by day.
Pure, pure was the love that her fair bosom held,
    And pure was the feeling that woke at her name;
But our own time has seen her devotion excelled,
    And her brightest fame darkened by Nightingale's fame.

It was not a lover whose pallet *she* smoothed,
  She plied not *her* task in a castle's proud room;
The poor wounded soldier she tended and soothed,
  'Mid the hospital's fetid and comfortless gloom!
She talked to him—dying—of life beyond earth,
  Till the soul passed, in joy, from the war-shattered frame;
And for *this* she had left her fair home and bright hearth!—
  O! Mortal ne'er merited Nightingale's fame!

The purest of earthly love ever is mixed
  With something of earth. On the one side all soul,
All sense on the other, it hovers betwixt,
  And—touching on both—bears a taint through the whole.
But *her* love was free from the human alloy;
  'Twas a flame from the Holiest's altar of flame!—
She went forth an Angel of Mercy and Joy,
  And Angels might covet our Nightingale's fame!

SEBASTOPOL IS LOW!

1855.

How eagerly we listen
   For the tidings which, we know,
Must thunder from the Euxine—
   Of the Russian's overthrow,
Of the struggle, of the carnage,
   Redly heaping friend on foe—
When the last assault is over
   And Sebastopol is low!

Think ye we fight for glory?
   We won it long ago!
Or for a wider empire?
   No—by our honour—no!
But we fight for FREEDOM's empire—
   And *that* shall wider grow,
When the last assault is over,
   And Sebastopol is low!

O'er the nations darkly pining
   In serfdom's night of woe,
See! the clouds are being scattered,
   And the dawn begins to glow!
And the lark of Freedom—singing—
   Through sunny skies shall go,
When the last assault is over,
   And Sebastopol is low!

Hark! heard ye not those boomings,
   Repeated deep and slow?
'Tis the voice of Freedom's triumph—
   It is struck—the glorious blow!
And all through merry England
   Brave songs, to-night, shall flow;
For the last assault *is* over,
   And Sebastopol *is* low!

THE ZEPHYR OF MAY.

1856.

A song of the Peace.

The spring will bring peace, as it brings the fine weather,
  The war and the winter will both have blown o'er;
And joys, like the flowers upon greensward and heather,
  Will bloom o'er the land in profusion once more.
Fair eyes, dim with weeping now, then will be bright again—
  No dewy violets brighter then they!
True hearts that are heavy now, then will be light again—
  Dancing like leaves in the zephyr of May!

Alas, there are hearts that, the higher our gladness,
  The deeper will sink in their fathomless woe;
There are eyes to which spring will bring nothing but sadness,
  Since it cannot bring those whom the war has laid low!

But God will pour balm into bosoms despairing;
　The Mourner, in time, will look upward and say—
" He died a brave death! he won peace by his daring!"
　And a proud sigh will blend with the zephyr of May.

With flag by foes riddled, but O! never captured,
　Our warriors will bound again o'er the sea-foam;
And the loved ones, left woful, will meet them, enraptured,
　And in triumph bear each to his now-honoured home.
We have proved to the world—and the world will remember—
　That to conquer in battle we still know the way!
But though we—to the foe—are the blast of December,
　We are—to the vanquished—the zephyr of May!

FORGIVE ME, O MY NATIVE HILLS!

1856.

[Written after visiting Alnwick Castle.]

Forgive me, O my native hills,
    Whose breezes fan my brow;
And O my native streams and rills,
    Forgive your Minstrel now!

A spell is working in my brain
    And overpowers your own,
Which fails to wake, or bring again,
    Emotions dead, or flown.

I do not in each lone place kneel,
    As I—aforetime—knelt;
I cannot gaze, I cannot feel,
    As then I gazed and felt.

On all your well-known forms I glance,
    Which yet I hardly view;
For still comes one sweet countenance
    Between my eyes and you!

It beams from Lanton's grassy hill,
 It glances from the Glen,
And in the Beaumont's mirror still
 It fades, and comes again!

'Tis in yon mist, which Newton Torr
 Now lowers, now updraws,
And lo! the mist is mist no more—
 But Beauty's veil of gauze!

Forgive me! Ye are still my pride,
 Your charms I still prefer;
But now my soul will not divide
 The worship due to HER,

Who charms by condescension, yet
 Ne'er seems to condescend;
In whom are all the graces met,
 And all the virtues blend:

Who in her halls, but yesterday,
 Received your humble bard,
And deigned some words of praise to say,
 Each word—a life's reward!

A BEING THERE IS.

1857.

—

A Being there is, of whose endless existence,
   No sane mind e'er doubted, or harboured a doubt;
A Being with whom there is no time, no distance;
   Who pervades all within me, pervades all without.

In my brain, at this instant, He marks every motion
   Of thought—as if no thought were moving but mine;
Yet sees, the same instant, each whim and each notion
   In every quick brain from the poles to the line!

Nor, while He is watching Earth's myriads, can it
   Be said that from any one orb He is far;
No, He is as near to yon beautiful planet,
   His essence imbosoms the furthest lone star!

The furthest lone star? It is language that labours—
   No star is, to Him, either furthest or lone;
And the star we deem lone, may have millions of neighbours,
   Whose beams ne'er have yet through our atmosphere shone!

These love-peopled worlds are the bright emanation
  Of goodness yet brighter, which words would but
    dim;
And the meanest intelligent life in creation,
  Hath the care, the protection, the kindness of Him!

If we think that He leaves us, we then are forgetting
  That He is the fixed, the unchangeable One—
The sun leaves not us, when it seems to be setting,
  'Tis we who are turning away from the sun!

OUR SAXON FATHERS!

1858.

[Set to music by G. W. Marten. Published in the Journal of Part Music, and recently performed in Exeter Hall by the National Choral Society.—ED.]

Our Saxon fathers built a bridge
  With piers and arches massive,
Which now hath stood for many a year
  To flow and flood impassive.
From every treacherous inland foe,
  From every bold sea-rover,
It was their pride and boast to guard
  The bridge that bore them over.

The Norman clutched it; but the pride
   Our sires had learned to cherish,
Disdained submission, and they swore
   To win it back or perish.
They met in arms at Runnymede,
   Prepared to stain the clover,
Had not the tyrant yielded up
   The bridge that bore them over.

The Stuart seized it for himself,
   And from the people blocked it;
He on the centre placed a gate,
   And trebly barred and locked it.
The people rose. A thunder-cloud
   Seemed o'er the place to hover,
Then burst!—and gate and block had left
   The bridge that bore them over.

Time weareth all. Some rifts may claim
   A wise examination,
A stone decayed may be replaced;
   Not touched the old foundation!
O let us swear—hand locked in hand
   From John o'Groat's to Dover—
To keep, 'gainst home and foreign foes,
   The bridge that bears us over!

VERSES.

1858.

[Recited at the Freemasons' Tavern, London, on the occasion of the celebration of the DUKE OF NORTHUMBERLAND'S birth-day, the 15th December.—ED.]

WE come not here all selfishly,
   From sense of favours shown;
For *that* too independent, we
   A nobler impulse own.
We come to pay such homage here
   As honest men may pay
To ONE they honour and revere,
   On this his natal day!

To flatter greatness which is based
   On rank and wealth alone—
Why, we should feel ourselves disgraced,
   Although it filled a throne;
But when 'tis based on native worth,
   And shines with native rays,
We then were "earthy—of the earth,"
   If we forbore to praise!

And here no flower of song there needs ;
    For all our hearts attest,
That but to simply state his deeds,
    Would be to praise him best.
But who, in tracing back the past,
    Can half his deeds compute,
Whose sympathies embrace the vast,
    And touch the most minute!

Whate'er in science and in art
    Exalts his native land,
He cherishes with hand and heart—
    Warm heart, and open hand.
Where'er song blooms, like vernal shower
    His patronage distils,
Down to the very lowliest flower
    That decks Northumbrian hills!

The sailor, far on ocean's foam,
    For him bids prayer ascend;
The little swimmer, nearer home,
    Knows well his princely friend.
When o'er the coasting vessel's deck
    Hath burst th' engulphing wave,
A beacon to the humblest wreck
    'Tis his to shine and save.

While his ancestral Towers receive
  Fresh grandeur from his taste,
No poor man's dwelling will he leave
  To Time's incessant waste.
Proud to adorn—as who would not?—
  The home that HOTSPUR knew,
He loves to give the peasant's cot
  Its meet adornment too.

Means all but boundless *others* boast—
  Who boasts, like him, a Mind
That studies how his wealth shall most
  And best befriend mankind?
And be his FAIRER SELF named here—
  No deed we justly laud
He ever does, but *she* is near,
  To prompt it, or applaud!

Then to his health a bumper fill!
  And when the glass we raise,
We *feel* that, praise him as we will,
  We cannot over-praise.
And when—long hence!—he quits life's walk,
  Life's duties nobly done,
A far Posterity shall talk
  Of GOOD DUKE ALGERNON!

BURNS' CENTENARY FESTIVAL,
AN ODE.

[Written expressly for, and recited at, the Alloway Festival, in "Burns' Cottage," 25th January, 1859.]

I.

What moves fair Scotland? Tell me why
    Her realm of old renown
Hears everywhere one festive cry
    In country and in town?
What stirs her peasantry, that they
    The long procession crowd?
And what hath mixed with their array
    The high-born and the proud?
Wherefore hath Science poured her sons
    To swell and grace the throng?
And Poesy her noblest ones
    That charm the land with song?
Tell me what cause together brings
    A Nation's wealth and worth?
Commemorate they the birth of Kings?
    No, no! a PEASANT's birth!

II.

A PEASANT! born to teach the great
    That, honoured as they are,
There may be found in low estate
    Men—their superiors far;

And that while Royalty transmutes
　　Liegemen to lords at will,
NATURE selects and institutes
　　A Peerage grander still!
To teach the patient sons of toil
　　That they have *that* within,
Which makes the Tillers of the soil
　　And all above them, kin;
That they are born with rights to scan,
　　And, if need be, to save;
That each—the least—is still a Man
　　Whom none dare make a slave;
That though the accident of birth
　　A different rank hath given,
They have with them a common earth,
　　With them, a common Heaven!
— High teachings! and exemplified
　　On many a Scottish sward,
Where rich and poor, with equal pride,
　　Applaud their Peasant-Bard!

III.

Not mournfully—as if his death
　　Were still a recent woe—
We mingle where he first drew breath
　　A hundred years ago;
Not mournfully, but joyfully,
　　Exultingly we meet—
Above our heads his " lift sae hie,"
　　His land beneath our feet!

Ay, his! for time—whate'er beside
    Its ravage overturns—
Will leave this land its name of pride,
    "The Land of ROBERT BURNS!"
His! for your bard was not of those
    Bright meteors—brief as bright;
The Light that erst in Ayrshire rose
    Is an undying Light!
'Tis burning, shining,—shedding still,
    Where'er its beam extends,
A brighter tint on vale and hill
    Than fairest sunshine lends!
His! for the King of Scottish song
    His Banner here unfurled;
And round it now—as subjects—throng
    The men that move the world!

IV.

O enviable Triumph! Nor
    To Scotland now confined—
The Peasant-Bard, your own no more,
    Belongs to all mankind!
Veiled in the tongue which many a strain
    To every Scot endears,
But which, till BURNS began his reign,
    Was strange to Southern ears—

Veiled in the language of the North,
    His genius burst its shroud,
Like sunshine from the cloud went forth—
    The brighter for the cloud!
And now his words—each word a ray—
    O'er earth their splendours dart,
But win their first and easiest way
    To ENGLAND's sister heart.
His love of right, his hate of wrong,
    His quenchless freedom-thirst,
Which made this bard of burning song
    Of Freedom's bards the First—
His lays on woman fair and pure,
    Our best gift from above,
Which ever will his rank insure,
    First of the bards of Love—
Find *there* congenial feelings rife
    That burn and bind till death,
Where LOVE is held the soul of life,
    And LIBERTY the breath!

V.

O Triumph dearly purchased! Ye
    Who garnish now his tomb,
And—pondering on the misery
    Which closed his early doom—

Are prone to say "If we had been
    Existent in his day,
We would not, like our sires, have seen
    The bard *so* pass away!"
More humbly think, nor harshly blame
    What seems indeed a crime—
Ye view him in the light of fame,
    And through the haze of time;
Ye care not now the faults to see
    With which his life was charged,
And which a dull malignity
    Then blackened and enlarged;
Nor can ye tell how few of those
    Who might have sought his weal,
Were ever cognizant of woes
    His Pride would not reveal.
Then gently blame, if blame ye must,
    But, first, inquire with care,
Are *ye* to Living Worth more just
    Than your forefathers were?
Go—if ye slight your gifted ones
    Till quenched their sacred fires,
Go—earn that censure from your sons
    Ye lavish on your sires!

VI.

I leave his woes. The Muse's gold
    Is ever tried by fire;
In suffering she is wont to mould
    Her Masters of the lyre.

And who would shun his woes, could he
  Secure the fruit they bore—
His country's love from sea to sea,
  And fame for evermore!
I leave his faults. To dwell on them
  Good men will little reck;
The brighter that we find the gem,
  The darker seems the speck.
And thousands pass—unblamed—from sight,
  Far deeplier stained than He,
Whose genius yields, itself, the light
  By which the stains we see!

VII.

Nor will I seek, presumptuously,
  The curtain to updraw
Which covers that ETERNITY
  No mortal ever saw.
But I—for one—will ne'er believe
  That his Great Heart which, here,
Was formed to grieve with those that grieve,
  And longed to dry each tear!—
Which loved the true, the pure, the good,
  In cottage or in hall,
And sang, in many a glorious mood,
  The loves and joys of all!—
Which hated all things bad and base,
  All fraud and falsehood spurned,
And 'gainst th' Oppressors of his race
  Its keenest arrows turned!—

Which warmly felt, and widely poured,
  The freeman's, patriot's flame,
Till Scotland grew a " household word"
  Extensive as his fame !—
I never will believe that—beat
  That Great Heart where it may—
It beats in aught but BLISS COMPLETE,
  In GOD's eternal day !

VIII.

O pause !—We know not what new powers
  Departed spirits gain,
Nor whether with this world of ours
  Their sympathies remain ;
But if remembrance do survive
  The severance from the clay ;
If feelings, ruling when alive,
  Retain their wonted sway ;
If souls have consciousness on high
  Of things that here take place,
And, with invigorated eye,
  Can dart their glance through space ;—
Who knows ! OUR POET now may bend
  His eye on scenes like this,
And SCOTIA's gathered homage lend
  A heart-swell e'en in bliss !

THAT BEAUTIFUL THOUGHT!

1860.

(Probably the last written poetry by Story.—ED.)

"That beautiful thought!" I exclaimed, as I mused
   Beneath a spring sky, with a moon full and bright,
And as a thought—new, or if not so, unused—
   Glanced into my soul from the grandeur of Night!

"That beautiful thought!" O! if now I had words
   Of music to fix it in measure and rhyme,—
Like the often-heard, joy-giving song of the birds
   It might be a pleasure for all coming time!

"As it is, it will lie, like a grain from ripe ears,
   In the soil of my mind, nor may ever unfold;
Or if ever—long hence, in the passage of years,—
   But where—Ah me!—where are the years to the old?"

The "Ah me!" was a sigh for my life in the wane,
   Worn to its last round, to re-brighten no more—
And for the slight chance that aught new in my brain
   Would e'er find expression in verse, as of yore.

For my songs have—the most of them—not sprung at once
    From the fancy or feeling that prompted them first;
Which lay stored in my breast—till in ready response
    To some impulse of power—into numbers it burst.

" But *shall* this thought perish," I cried, though to me
    Come never the mood that would wake it to birth?
The *something* which thinks, shall it e'er cease to be?
    Or cease to remember its musings on earth?

" O! may not I yet—out of clay, out of time—
    Enriched with new language, endowed with new powers,
Remember this thought in the fair spirit-clime,
    And sing it to angels in amaranth-bowers?

" And O! may not thoughts—new, and beauteous as new—
    Flowing still into song as in life they have flowed,
Make my Time's dearest joy my Eternity's too—
    Song—song—ever fresh—in the realms of my God!"

LIST OF SUBSCRIBERS.

	Plain.	Gilt.
His Grace the Duke of Northumberland, K.G.		6
Her Grace the Duchess of Northumberland		6
Her Grace the Dowager Duchess of Northumberland		4
The Right Hon. the Earl de Grey and Ripon		2
The Right Hon. Lord Wharncliffe		2
Sir Thomas Acland, Bart., Killerton, Devon		2
Sir W. C. Trevelyan, Bart., Wallington		2

	Plain	Gilt
Alcock, W. N., Newfield Hall, Skipton	10	
Alderson, Mr., Northumberland House, London		1
Atterbury, W. S., 4, Paddington Green, do.		1
Atkinson, J., Settle	1	
Alison, Dr. Scott, Park St., Grosvenor Sq., L'don	1	
Ackroyd, Geo., North Park Villas, Bradford		1
Atlee, Henry, Isleworth, Middlesex	1	
Avery, Robert, North Shields	1	
Bagster, George, Audit Office, London		1
Brent, Algernon, do. do.		1
Bathurst, W. H. D., do. do.	1	
Bishop, J. D., do. do.	1	
Bristow, Mr., Hounslow, Middlesex		1
Bartholomew, Mr., Brentford, do.		1
Buckmaster, Mr., New Road, Battersea	1	
Bosworth & Harrison, Regent Street, London.	4	

LIST OF SUBSCRIBERS.

	Plain.	Gilt.
Bradley, George, Guardian Office, Newcastle	1	
Bond, Mr., 176, Oxford Street, London	2	
Brown, Henry, Gilling Lodge, Hampstead		1
Bailey, Mr., High Holborn, London	1	
Bray, J., Marsh Lane, Battersea	1	
Begbie, C., 10, Coleman Street, London		1
Blackwell, Mr., Brentford End, Middlesex	1	
Bailey, Mr., Manchester	1	
Barton, Mr., 3, Strand, London		1
Byfield, Messrs. 21, Charing Cross, London	1	1
Box, A. V., Brentford, Middlesex		1
Burrow, Matthew C., Tatham, near Settle	1	
Beach, J., Surgeon, Bradford	1	
Briggs, Hickson, Isleworth, Middlesex		1
Badham, George, Birmingham		1
Barker, Wm., Railway Engineer, Bradford	1	
Barret, E. A., Solicitor, do.		1
Birkbeck, T., Tauntfield, Taunton		2
Birkbeck, J., Ingfield, Settle		1
Bremner, S., Belle Sauvage Printg. Wks., London		1
Burrow, Rev. R. J., High Bentham, Settle	1	
Battersby, J., Settle	1	
Bolam, John, Alwinton, Northumberland		1
Bayliss, Mr., Twickenham		1
Bowyer, Mr., do.		1
Crossley, Frank, M.P., Belle Vue, Halifax.		1
Crossley, John, Dean Clough Mills, do.	1	
Curzon, Hon. H. Roper, Audit Office, London		1
Coldicott, S. O., do. do.		1
Campbell, H., do. do.	1	
Crisp, Mrs., Bow St., Covent Garden, do.		1
Crisp, Miss, 168, New Bond Street, do.		1
Cockford, Mrs., do.		1
Cawthorne & Hutt, Cockspur Street, do.	6	
Cheeswas, Mr., Twickenham	1	
Cooper, P., Canonbury	1	
Cunningham, R., Frederick Place, London	4	

LIST OF SUBSCRIBERS.

	Plain.	Gilt.
Carr, Rev. H. B., Whickham, Gateshead		1
Carr, Ralph, Hedgeley, Alnwick		1
Cuthbert, Mrs., Northumberland House, London		1
Colls, L., 168, New Bond Street, London		1
Clarkson, Thos., East Cowton, Northallerton		1
Charlton, Dr., 7, Eldon Square, Newcastle	1	
Clark, Robert, Grove Hill, Canterbury		6
Clark, Rev. J. D., the Hall, Belford		1
Crighton, Edwin, North Shields		1
Dickson, William, Alnwick		6
Day, H. G., Isleworth, Middlesex		1
Dixon, Mr., 21, Cockspur Street, London		1
Drake, Mr., Staines, Middlesex	1	
Dunn, Rev. J. W., Warkworth	1	
Delaunay, F. W., Architect, Bradford	1	
Drummond, Edmund, Audit Office, London	1	
Dugnall, Edward, Oak Terrace, Battersea		1
Dodd, J. P., LL.D., North Shields	1	
Dodd, P. A., Howard Street, do.	1	
Davis, Miss, M. E., Brighton		1
Dicken, Mr., Brentford End, Middlesex		1
Davison, A., Hastings Cottage, Seaton Delaval		1
Edwards, Charles, Tunbridge Wells	1	
East, Joshua, Curzon Street, May Fair		1
Elphick, Mrs., Mount Lebanon, Twickenham		1
Farrer, J., M.P., Ingleborough House, Settle		1
Firth, George, Merchant, Bradford		10
Farnell, James, Isleworth, Middlesex		1
Farnell, Charles, do. do.		1
Farnell, Henry, do. do.		1
Farnell, W. T., do. do.		1
Farnell, John, do. do.		1
Fox, Mr., Camden Row Villas, do.	1	
Feetham, Mr., 9, Clifford Street, London	.2	
Finch, G., Solicitor, Oak House, Battersea	2	

LIST OF SUBSCRIBERS.

	Plain.	Gilt.
Faitland, T., Settle	..	1
Fenwick, W., Bloomfield	1	
Foster, J. W., Settle	..	1
Foster, E. T., do.	..	1
Fyfe, T., 6, Holbury Street, Chelsea	1	
Fabian, James, Portland Place, London	1	
Fenwick, J. F., M.D., Bolton	1	
Fawens, William, North Shields	1	
Grey, Jno., Dilston, Northumberland	..	2
Groves, Mr., 33, Charing Cross, London	1	
Goodman, H. J., 3, Langham St., London	1	
Garrard, Sebastian, 25, Haymarket, do.	1	
Gooden, H., 14, Noel Street do.	1	
Gardner, J. E., St. John's Wood Park, do.		1
Giles, Jno., Brentford		1
Galpin, T. D., Belle Sauvage Printg.Wks. London		1
Geller, W. O., Stanhope Place, London		1
Graigg, H. A., Kirkby Lonsdale	1	
Glover, Alderman, South Shields	1	
Greenwell, W., North Shields		1
Gawthorp, Mr., 48, Charles St., Westminster		1
Goodenough, Mr., Isleworth	1	
Goswell, Mr., Twickenham		1
Gibbison, Mrs., Mount Lebanon, do.	1	
Greenwood, Richd., Solicitor, Gargrave		1
Henderson, J., 42, Windmill Street, London	1	
Henderson, Wm., do. do.	..	2
Harrison, William, Surgeon, Gargrave		1
Hartley, G., Settle		1
Hartley, W., do.	1	
Hartley, J. J., do.	1	
Hartley, Mrs., Lion Hotel, Settle	1	
Hodges, Edward, Wigmore Street, London	1	
Harris, H., Heaton Hall, Bradford	..	3
How, J., 7, Upper Marylebone St., London	1	
Hayday, Mr., 31, Little Queen St., do.	1	
Hammond, J., 15, Noel St., Soho, do.	1	

LIST OF SUBSCRIBERS.

	Plain.	Gilt.
Harrison, Mr., 25, Haymarket, London	1	
Hirst, L., Audit Office, do.		1
Hill, George, 387, Oxford Street, do.	1	
Hill, Robert, Halifax	1	
Hedley, George, Artist, Halifax	1	
Holme, D. M., Milne Garden, Coldstream	1	
Howard, Wm., 2, Hanway St., London	1	
Hooper, Mr., 28, Haymarket, do.	1	
Hall, Henry, Clitheroe	1	
Hirst, Mrs., 2, Hyde Lane, Battersea		1
Hobbs, S., Surrey Lane, do.		1
Hardy, E. T., Bridge Road, do.		1
Hillier, W., 6, Middleton Terrace, Battersea		1
Hitchcock, S. E., do. do.		1
Hunter, Mr., Alnwick	1	
Henderson, John, Glasgow	1	
Hunter, T. S., Granton Pier, Edinburgh	1	
Hudson, Thomas, North Shields	1	
Haswell, T., do.	1	
Hubble, Mrs., Chigwell Row, London		2
Hillhouse, Mr., 11, New Bond St., London		1
Hammond, W. S., 14, Noel St., Soho, do.		1
Hulbert, Mr., Isleworth		1
Hiscock, Mr., Hounslow		1
Holroyd, A., Bookseller, Bradford	1	
Hardcastle, C. D., College St., Keighley		1
Hawksworth, Peter, Woolstapler, Bradford	1	
Hedley, Thos., Coslodge, Newcastle-on-Tyne		1
Hedley, Saml., do.		1
Ingleby, C., Harden Cottage, Clapham		1
Iveson, Mrs. E., Brentford End, Middlesex	1	
Ingledew, H., Mayor of Newcastle-on-Tyne		1
Ingram, Rev. Robert, Chatburn		2
Ingledew, C.J.D., M.A., PH.D., F.G.H.S., Northallerton	1	
Illingworth, Henry, Solicitor, Bradford	1	
Jardine, Sir W., Bt., Jardine Hall, Dumfries	1	

LIST OF SUBSCRIBERS.

	Plain.	Gilt.
Jackson, Miss Mary, Kingstown, Ireland		1
Jenkinson, Rev. S. J., Vicar, Battersea		1
Johnston, James, Pimlico, London		2
Johnson, T. M., Eshton, Skipton		2
Jackson, Mr., Twickenham		1
Judson, Wm., Syon House, Middlesex	1	
Jackson, Henry, 315, Oxford Street, London	1	
Jones, Mr., 194, Piccadilly, do.		1
Jones, Mrs., Twickenham, Middlesex	1	
Keen, Mr., Isleworth, Middlesex	1	
Keen, Miss L., Green Lane, Battersea	1	
Keith, Alex., Audit Office, London		1
Knight, Mrs., Bridge End, Battersea		1
Karr, Jas., Roxburgh Lodge, London	1	
Kelly, Jas., Kingston-upon-Thames	1	
Kirkman, John, 76, Bolsover St., London	1	
Kay, Mr., Thornton	1	
Laing, John, Western Hill, Durham	1	
Laing, W., 3, Adelaide Terrace, Newcastle		1
Langthorne, James, 160, Piccadilly, London		1
Lanceley, W., East Smithfield, do.		1
Lancaster, Wm., Solicitor, Bradford	1	
Lovegrove, Mr., Twickenham, Middlesex		1
Lumpus, Robert, Isleworth, do.	1	
Lockit, Mr., Northumberland Wharf, London		2
Lyall, Geo., Winchester St., South Shields	1	
Lock, Robert, Hollington Lodge, Sussex		3
Lewis, W., Surgeon, Paddington St. London	1	
Lockwood, R., 2, Burwood Place, do.	1	
Lockwood, John, do. do.		1
Leathart, Mr., Newcastle-on-Tyne		1
Lister, John, Settle	1	
Mitford, Hon. Miss, Vernon House, London	1	
Martin, J. E., Inner Temple Library, do.		1
Mawley, H., 20, Gower Street, do.		1
Mitchell, Mr., Argyle Street, do.		1

LIST OF SUBSCRIBERS.

	Plain.	Gilt.
Mackintosh, Mr., 37, Langham St., London	1	
Mackinlay, Jno., M.D., Isleworth, Middlesex	1	
Montrie, Mr., 55, Baker Street, London	1	
Macdonald, Wm., do.	1	
Mackay, Wm., King Street, South Shields	1	
Miles, John, Brentford, Middlesex		1
May, Mr., Twickenham, do.		1
Mortimer, Mrs., Syon House, do.	1	
Morgan, John, Brentford End, do.	1	
Milligan, H., Benton Park, Bradford		1
Mallet, Charles, Audit Office, London		1
Markby, Montague do. do.		1
Marshall, Capt., Wray, Lancashire		1
Mason, Joseph, Grassington Hall, Skipton		2
Meade, R. H., Surgeon, Bradford		1
Nicholson, H. W., Berkhampstead		6
Noble, Mr., 13, Charing Cross, London		1
Naylor, W., Manor House, Paddington Gn.		2
Nicholas, N. H., Audit Office, London		1
North, C., Chelsea		1
Nowell, M., Blackburn	1	
Nicholson, T., Kirkgate, Bradford	1	
Oriel, S. F., Audit Office, London		1
Orde, Robert, Grasse Cottage, London	4	
Oliver, W., John St., Tottenham Court Road	1	
Preston, Miss, Flasby Hall, Skipton		2
Plummer, John, Kettering		1
Pollard, J. P., Upper John Street, London	4	1
Preston, J., Settle		1
Parker, John, Bowling, Bradford		1
Pengilly, Miss A., Windmill St., London		1
Pearce, Utting, 17, London Street, do.		1
Perry, William, London		1
Poupart, Mr., Battersea Fields, London		1
Page, Mr., Twickenham, Middlesex		1

LIST OF SUBSCRIBERS.

	Plain.	Gilt.
Price, Mr., Twickenham, Middlesex		1
Powell, Mr., do. do.		1
Peisley, Mr., Hounslow, do.		1
Quinion, Mr., do. do.		1
Richards, Geo., Palace Garden Terrace, Kensington	1	
Rea, Charles, Doddington, Wooler		1
Rea, Mr., Nun's Street, Newcastle-on-Tyne	1	
Robinson, H. J., Brentford, Middlesex	1	
Rogers, W. P., Blackheath		1
Ramsden, Henry, Dentist, Bradford	1	
Robinson, Wm., Settle		1
Redmayne, T., Taitlands, Settle		1
Robinson, Dixon, Clitheroe		1
Robinson, Arthur, Blackburn		1
Roper, R., Kirkby Lonsdale	1	
Robertson, Thomas, Alnwick	1	
Rogers, John, 7, Cleveland Street, London		1
Rogers, Stephen, do. do.		1
Rogers, Mr., 24, Bow Street, do.		1
Randall, Joseph, 45, Marshall St., do.		1
Reaney, J. L., George Hotel, Bradford		1
Ridley, John, King Street, North Shields	1	
Salt, Titus, Methley Hall, near Leeds	12	
Seager, Mr., Isleworth	1	
Shepherd, E. W., Audit Office, London		1
Shaw, Dr., Portland House, Battersea		1
Smith, Mr., Syon House, Middlesex	1	
Smith, Mark, Bookseller, Alnwick,	2	
Smith, W., Farnborough Terrace, London	1	
Smith, George, 43, Wimpole St., do.		3
Swail, J. C., Hammersmith, do.	1	1
Surman, A., Mount Lebanon, Twickenham		1
Stoothen, J., North Shields	1	
Simms, Richard, do.	1	
Smart, R. T., 3, Russell Crescent, London		1

LIST OF SUBSCRIBERS.

	Plain	Gilt
Segnier, Mr., 3, Russell Crescent, London		1
Spedwell, Mr., Twickenham, Middlesex		1
Storey, John, Manchester		1
Storey, T., Grey St., Newcastle-on-Tyne	1	
Storey, Mrs. W., Rye Hill, do.	1	
Storey, Mr., Somerset House,	1	
Stead, Mr., Chelsea		1
Schlesinger, Martin, Newcastle-on-Tyne	1	
Searcey, Mr., 19, Upper Berkeley St., London	2	
Starkie, Mr., 4, Strand, do		1
Stirling, T. H., High Street, Battersea		1
Short, Miss, Wooler, Northumberland	1	
Schmedlin, F. X., 6, Russell Place, London	1	
Soden, Jonathan, 18, Langham Pl., do.	1	
Sampson, W., 19, Queen's Terrace, Bayswater	1	
Stanfield, C., Bradford	1	
Simpson, W. G., Newcastle-on-Tyne	1	
Talbot, Hon. Mrs. R. G., Ballinclea House, Kingstown, Ireland		1
Taylor, R., 4, Adelaide Pl., London Bridge	1	
Taylor, R., Jun., 11, Terrace, Kennington Pk.		2
Taylor, G., Scotland Yard, London		2
Taylor, John, Wraysbury, Bucks	1	
Thomas, H., Prescot Cottage, Battersea		1
Thornton, Mrs. B., (late Miss Reaney) Harrogate		20
Thick, T., Brentford End, Middlesex	1	
Tolson, Mrs., Crow Trees, Bradford		1
Tucker, Mr., Bankruptcy Office, Newcastle		1
Trumper, R., Brentford end, Middlesex	1	
Thomas, W., 29, Berners St., London	1	
Tripp, Mr., Manchester Square, do.	1	
Turnham, Geo., do. do.	1	
Turner, Mr., 31, Haymarket, do.	1	
Twopenny, W., Lambs Buildings do.		1
Thompson, John, Alnwick	1	
Tasker, J. and Son, Skipton	1	
Turnbull, Thomas do.	1	

LIST OF SUBSCRIBERS.

	Plain.	Gilt.
Tate, Rev. W. G. do.		1
Valle, Barte, 31, Haymarket, London		1
Warrington, Mr., 27, Strand, London	1	
Williams, Thos., Northumberl'd House, do.		4
Williams, Mr., 12, Lansdowne Terrace, do.	1	
Williams, Henry, Brentford, Middlesex		1
Watson, Jos., Langham Street, London		1
Watson, W. P., Isleworth, Middlesex		1
Watson, T., Brompton, do		1
Walters, T., 5, Albany Road, London		1
Willans, Mr., Crowley Lock, Uxbridge	1	
Watkins, C., Brentford End, Middlesex	1	
Wing, Mr., Isleworth, do.	1	
Wells, A., Kingston-upon-Thames	1	
Webster, J., Solicitor, Sheffield		1
Wilson, F. R., Architect, Alnwick	1	
Wanless, W., Richmond, Yorkshire	1	
Wildman, C., 2, Princess Street, London		1
Wilkinson, Mr., Old Bond St., do.		1
Wilkinson, J., Bentham, Settle	1	
Wright, Rev. J. M., Rectory, Tatham, Settle		1
Watkinson, S., Highgate House, Gargrave		1
Walker, Mr., Percy's Works, Newcastle		1
White, Mr., Elm Tree House, do.		1
Woods, M., 18, Eldon Square, do.		1
Wonacott, W., Portland Street, London	1	
Watts, T., 22, Up.Marylebone St. do.	1	
Wright, J., North Shields	1	
Waddell, Rev. J. H., Girvan Ldge., Ayrshire		1
Whitmore, Mr., 45, Charles St., Westminster		1
Wood, Mr., Hounslow		1
Wall, Mr., Richmond, Surrey		1
Wigglesworth, Jas., Valley Road, Bradford	1	
Wentworth, F. W., Wentworth Castle, Barnsley		1
Young, Charles, North Shields		1

www.ingramcontent.com/pod-product-compliance
Lightning Source LLC
Chambersburg PA
CBHW030816230426
43667CB00008B/1236